Foreword by Issata O.

WHAT
MAKES
GEN-Z
DIFFERENT?

BEN SEYI-OLA
Afterword by Dr. Amos Fenwa

DISCLAIMER

The names of certain individuals and their identifying details have been changed to protect their privacy. Therefore, all names, characters, places, incidents, and other entities are fictitious. Any resemblance to actual people, living or dead, or actual events is purely coincidental.

The information provided in this book is **not an attempt to practice medicine or give specific medical advice, including, but not limited to, advice about mental health.**

The information contained in this book is for the sole purpose of being informative and is not to be considered complete. It does not cover all issues related to mental health.

This information is not a replacement for consultation with your doctor or other qualified mental health providers and/or specialists. Also, this book is not intended to be a source of financial or legal advice. Making adjustments to a financial strategy or plan should only be undertaken after consulting with a professional.

To Joy!

Connect with Ben Seyi-Ola
by scanning the QR code below

Be greater than
& soar higher!

DEDICATION

To Dorcas Ola, my best co-pilot who has journeyed with me to raise our children, thank you. I am grateful that we are parents to beautiful Gen-Z and Gen-Alpha children.

To the parents and guardians that I have worked with over the past 20 years, it's always my pleasure to work with you and your kids.

FOREWORD

I first met Ben during one of his initial visits to the United States. A kind, tall man with a gentle disposition whose teaching resonated with me as a public intellectual. Over time, I would have the privilege of working alongside Ben as we cultivated talent amongst teens and young adults. I also consider him a trusted mentor.

Gen Z can be incredibly challenging to engage. They are smart, computer-savvy, and accustomed to having access to information at their fingertips. Everything you do and say can be fact-checked within a matter of minutes. They are also quite leery of authority and leadership. To successfully engage them, you must come across as dependable but not bossy, educated but not elitist, and most importantly, trustworthy.

As a colleague and mentee of Ben Seyi-Ola, I can tell you firsthand that you have encountered a master speaker, teacher, and mentor to the gifted and talented. His leadership has challenged me to go from good to great in my character, ministry, and business endeavors. His consistency is unmatched, and his commitment to seeing young people excel is genuine and sincere.

In the pages of this book, Ben Seyi-Ola decodes one of the most complex generations that ever existed—Generation Next, a generation of forward-thinking, justice-oriented, and creative beings. As a senior leader in higher education, I am constantly challenged to increase in wisdom, transparency, and excellence as I work alongside GEN Z, something Ben Seyi-Ola has mastered in theory and practice. I highly recommend this book to any leader or parent seeking to maximize the potential of Gen Z.

-Issata O.
Associate Dean & Youth Mentor

TABLE OF CONTENTS

INTRODUCTION

Twenty-five years ago, I ventured into my private practice as a mentor and coach. Since then, I've worked with, trained, and mentored hundreds of the next generation. I'm still working with a few of them at the moment. I have three beautiful children, two of whom are in Generation Z. One is 17 years old and the other is 15 years old as of 2022 (the time of writing).

I work with parents and guardians of this younger generation on various matters—career, relationships, finances, and several other aspects. I help them understand how best to interact with and to oversee their children or wards.

While I was at university, I met someone. His name is Edward. We became very close friends. After my university days, we luckily settled in the same state. So, sometimes I met with him on my way to work and we would spend some time talking. Our friendship continued to blossom.

At the time I began my profession as a life coach and mentor, he was a naval officer; a well-respected, considerate, and highly skilled one. Edward was well known in his department. I recall thinking, "He's one of the good ones."

Three years ago, during my birthday celebration, Edward paid me a visit. He was with his son named Jerry, who was a couple of years older than my first son. His physique could make you mistake him for an adult. Edward had previously mentioned that he needed to schedule a meeting with me to see Jerry. So I was already looking forward to meeting him.

Jerry was a typical Generation Z who was trying to find himself. When he visited my home, I observed how he interacted with guests. After the party, we agreed on a day to meet. Jerry was a child born out of wedlock, and Edward and his wife had been trying to conceive since they got married, but to no avail. For a long time, Jerry was the only child in the family. Eventually, they conceived. But once they did, there was a shift of attention from Jerry to the newborn.

Edward brought Jerry to the meeting as scheduled. He also came with his wife, Jerry's stepmother. He had kept assuring his wife that Jerry would return to his normal self, but over time, things got worse. Hence, Edward sought professional help by consulting me. It was during the session that he filled me in on the current state of his relationship with his son.

When Jerry turned seventeen, Edward said he began to notice that some of the punishments that had worked in the past, like stern warnings, timeouts, having his allowance cut, and so on, were no longer working.

He used to think that the outbursts were just part of being a teenager, but now they were happening more often and getting worse. There was more power tussling. Along with that, he and his wife appeared to constantly disagree on the appropriate response to his outbursts.

He recounted a recent incident of how he was walking by Jerry's room door on a certain afternoon when he heard him sobbing in his bedroom while speaking on the phone. He was concerned but unsure whether to go in and ask him what was wrong. Because of his unpredictable behavior lately, they had really grown apart, and their relationship had become very tense.

Edward revealed his genuine confusion, saying he has been wondering if this is how being a parent actually feels and how he truly believes there is a missing piece of the puzzle that he cannot put together.

Edward said when he eventually summoned courage and opened Jerry's room door, he was met with an angry stare and the following ensued:

Jerry had yelled at him and said some things to him that broke his spirit.

"It's all your fault that they left," Jerry retorted.

"What's wrong with you?" Edward quizzed.

"Why are you crying?"

"My mother died, and now my girlfriend has dumped me," Jerry snapped angrily and started crying hysterically.

As Edward ran towards him to hug him, Jerry pushed him away violently, shouting, "Stay away from me!"

He recalled nearly losing his balance as Jerry pushed him away. He walked out of his son's room in tears, distraught.

When Edward was done talking, he looked at his wife, and she had the same sad look on her face as he did.

I shifted my gaze to the monitor to look at Jerry, who was in the next room fiddling with a Rubik's cube. I took a deep breath and began perusing my notes.

Something was apparent with Jerry's age and behavioral pattern. Edward and his wife had a Gen Z in their hands. And many parents are like my friend Edward, perplexed and unskilled as to how to handle their Gen Zers.

Some of these Gen Zers aren't even unruly at home, but they have distanced themselves from their parents and would rather choose to be glued to their phones, interacting with friends online.

So, I told Edward what I would tell any other Gen Z parent. Gen Zers must be understood. You cannot approach this generation using previous or well-established methods of engaging young adults that were used for previous generations. To groom Generation Z, you must view the world through their eyes. This will make it easier for you to understand how they think and what would be the most effective way of communicating with, leading, and disciplining them.

If you have ever wondered, what is the right approach to take while dealing with Generation Z children so they can succeed in life and still have wonderful child-parent relationships? Then this book is for you.

In this book, I'll be sharing some of the things that have aided me in mentoring many parents and children. They are also methods I use in communicating with and grooming my children, two of whom belong to Generation Z.

This book presents a brand-new method for parenting that is supported by facts, research, and science. It is a toolbox—one that is so meticulously arranged to proffer practical solutions to address the difficulties of parenting Gen Z.

I have a private counseling forum for parents that I coach. And during one of our meetings, I realized that every parent needs a hands-on manual to help them train their Gen Z children. Hence, I decided to write this book.

Parenting can be dicey. I am aware that the best course of action for one child may not be the best course of action for another because each child is unique.

I am currently raising two Gen Z kids, so this is beyond a job for me; it's my everyday role.

Like a lot of other experienced parenting coaches, I have helped hundreds of people and families all over Africa and United States, including teachers, therapists, psychologists, parents, and parents-to-be.

I will be sharing how we can increase cooperation, reduce stress, fortify our relationships, and treat our Gen Z with the respect they deserve by learning to establish, state, and defend our boundaries through various forms of communication and discipline.

PART ONE

CHAPTER ONE
Generational Diversity

We live in a multigenerational society.

I was born more than forty years ago and I have grown up to observe the vast difference between my generation, my parents' and that of my children. The parents and other adult guardians who have come to me for counseling have shown that the generational difference is a major source of stress between the parents and these young adults. The majority of parents have trouble understanding their children. However, we often forget that our own parents had trouble understanding us too. This issue is a generational thing, and it is not peculiar to one generation.

Today, the word "generation" is frequently used in pop culture, politics, and in conversations about self-identity.

What does the word really mean?

When considering the concept of "generation," there are many different perspectives that can be taken into account. It is a sociological phrase that refers to getting to know various social groupings, but it may also be used to explore family ties in contexts such as a generation tree.

In any family, there are many generations living side by side. In terms of kinship, the relationship between a parent and a child is referred to as a generation. You are of the same generation as your brothers and cousins due to the fact that your parents belong to the generation that came before you, and your children will belong to the generation that comes after you. In the vast majority of families, all of the members have children (or grandchildren) at approximately the same time.

Typically, generations are defined by the period of time it takes for children to mature from infancy to adulthood. For example, it probably took your grandparents 20–40 years to "grow up" before they had your parents, and then your parents had to grow up too, within that number of years before they could have children of their own.

The concept of generations is approached somewhat differently by sociologists and their research. A group of people who were born around the same time, often within a 20-year span, are considered to be members of the same generation.

However, due to the fact that people of a generation usually go through significant life changes and experiences with specific historical events that go on to define their lives, generations hold a unique and important significance.

Sociologists actively research the differences between different generations in order to get to some very major findings, and there is a lot that we can learn about our common experiences from these researchers.

The most recent generational categories were provided by the Pew Research Center, which describes itself as a nonpartisan think tank that informs the public about the issues, attitudes, and trends shaping the world.

The dates and events that define each generation can still help us understand our children, ourselves as parents, and why grandparents will always be perplexed by "children these days," regardless of the year. This is because the events and dates that define each generation have a way of resonating through time.

The following timeline illustrates the significant events that have occurred in each American generation since the year 1900, along with how those events have impacted both the children and the parents of that generation:

Born Between 1901 And 1924, Members Of The Greatest Generation (GI Generation)

Who exactly is a Gen GI?

Before enlisting in the armed forces to fight in World War II, members of this generation lived through the Great Depression.

Do not be misled by the wild provocations that were prevalent at the time in jazz and swing music; these musicians were notable for popularizing jazz.

Parents of the GI Generation, who had experienced the Great Depression, placed a premium on perseverance and hard work as a way to be successful in life.

Those Born Between 1928 And 1945 Are Members Of The Silent Generation.

Who are these people known as The Silent?

They became famous for being so submissive that during the McCarthy era, when the nation was paralyzed with dread of communism, they did not speak out against the government's policies.

Children were expected to develop a strong work ethic in order to achieve success in adulthood, which was consistent with the parenting philosophy of the time, which was similar to that of their parents.

Baby Boomers Are Individuals Whose Birth Years Range From 1946 To 1964

Who exactly are these baby boomers?

It's possible that Generation Z views Baby Boomers as their jaded grandparents ("Ok, Boomer"), but Baby Boomers actually had wild youths that weren't always spoken for. The term "boomers" originated to refer to the large number of children born in the United States after their parents returned from World War II. Baby Boomers disregarded their parents and participated in anti-Vietnam War demonstrations, which led to the birth of the "Summer of Love" movement.

The parenting styles of boomer parents were greatly altered as a result of the fact that they were the first generation to significantly consider their children's perspectives on growing up and to introduce the concept of family gatherings.

Birth Years For Generation X Range From 1965 To 1980

What exactly is meant by the term "Gen X"? The AIDS epidemic, the rise of MTV culture, and the beginning of the fight for LGBTQ+ rights were all things that Generation X, which is so often mocked as the "slacker generation," experienced.

Members of Generation X are credited with being the first parents to use the parenting style known as "helicopter parenting." Their Baby Boomer counterparts were notorious for allowing their children to play outside until the streetlights came on. Generation X parents, on the other hand, tend to be considerably more engaged in the social and academic development of their children than their Baby Boomer counterparts were.

Millennials Are Those Who Were Born Between 1981 And 1996

Who exactly are these Millennials? The Millennial generation is the first to have grown up both with and without the Internet throughout their formative years. As a result, the Internet now plays a significant role in the millennial generation's private lives. They were also alive during the events of September 11, 2001, and can remember when Amazon just sold books.

Despite accusations from Baby Boomers that Millennials are self-centered and entitled as a result of their excessive use of technology, Millennials have demonstrated that they are very community-oriented and ecologically sensitive. These characteristics are being adopted by their offspring—the generation that will follow them.

Who are the Millennials' parents? They are often known as perennials. Parents of children born in the millennial generation are succeeding in many endeavors, and in some ways, they may even be surpassing their predecessors. They are quite adaptable. According to experts, they are providing for the upbringing of their children in a wide variety of family ways.

They are more likely than parents of earlier generations to let their children completely express who they are and are leading the charge to assist children who identify as gender non-conforming. Some millennial parents, who themselves were "helicoptered over" as children, are now embracing a more permissive approach to parenting in which they provide their children with free opportunities for exploration and development.

Generation Z, Also Known As I Gen, Is Composed Of People Born Between 1997 And 2012

What is Gen Z? Children who are members of Generation Z are the first to be born into a world in which people are constantly connected to one another, even if this connection is maintained solely via the use of electronic devices such as smartphones and tablets.

> *Each generation goes further than the generation preceding it because it stands on the shoulders of that generation. You will have opportunities beyond anything we have ever known.*
>
> - Ronald Reagan

Which Generation Is Next?

In 2019, Adage categorized children born after 2010 as belonging to a generation known as Generation Alpha. Generation Alpha is the first generation of children who will have never known a period before social media, and as a result, they are expected to be substantially more technically skilled than prior generations. This is a great tool that has the capability of reshaping humanity in a number of constructive ways through a lot of different avenues.

In light of the fact that we know so little about the Alphas at the moment, it could be too soon to classify them as one thing or another.

However, there are a few aspects of them that we are aware of: They are more likely to live in households with only one parent than any other generation, and they have a greater likelihood of being afflicted by the COVID-19 epidemic than any other generation. They are also more diverse than any other generation.

The way that the culture perceives their generation will evolve with the passing of each year, just as it did for the generations who came before them. As their parents, we have the responsibility and the privilege of guiding them toward making the most responsible choices with the time that we have.

The features of a generation are not limited to the years in which its members were born. Other aspects of a person's life can have an effect on their birth cohort. The occurrences that took place afterwards also contribute to the generational definition.

Significant historical events have an impact on a generation.

Traditionalists, who were born between 1925 and 1945, experienced childhood through the Great Depression of the 1930s, in contrast to Baby Boomers, who were born between 1946 and 1964 and came of age during events such as the United States' landing on the moon and the Vietnam War.

In addition, Baby Boomers experienced the administrations of three different presidents and watched the assassinations of Reverend Martin Luther King, Jr., John F. Kennedy, and Robert F. Kennedy on television between the years 1961 and 1969.

The consequence of this was that these events left a mark on the behaviors, attitudes, and perceptions of Baby Boomers, pushing them to make changes in every aspect of American cultural life.

The inventions of technology have reshaped the world.

According to the traditionalists, the disruptive technologies were things like wireless radio, airplanes, and automobiles. In addition, the Baby Boomer generation was growing up at the same time that new technologies such as the transistor radio, audio cassette, and television were being introduced.

On the other hand, members of Generation X, who came of age during a time when personal computers and video cassette recorders were commonplace, had a totally different experience with technology in the United States.

Texting, emailing, utilizing social media, and using the Internet are all characteristics of the Millennial generation. In contrast, the Millennials are characterized by the use of personal computers, Xboxes, iPods, and DVD players. Due to the extensive adoption of digital technologies such as messaging apps, smartphones, tablets, and a variety of social media platforms, Gen Z can be differentiated from the generation that came before it.

During the first part of the 20th century, children who were growing up were accustomed to an educational atmosphere that was greatly influenced by military discipline. However, the conclusion of World War II brought about a change in learning techniques as well as learning environments. Baby Boomers received their education in classrooms that were orderly and silent.

When educators who were part of the Baby Boomer generation reached adulthood, they changed the rules and instituted a relaxed, round-table discussion structure for Generation X students.

As a result of advances in technology, Millennials are known for their multimodal learning environments, in which they blend their work, education, and fun activities.

The multi-stimulus world in which Generation Z is growing up, where adolescents and young people need the freedom to utilize a variety of gadgets and the ability to handle numerous conversations while learning, working, and playing, has been inspired by this type of learning style.

CHAPTER TWO
Gen Z: The Gen Y Apple

I'm not shocked that many adults don't understand the Gen Z generation.

Aside from the fact that they were born when technology was accessible to them, little is known about this generation.

They are the generation that comes after the Millennials, and some words we can use to characterize them include cheerful, positive, realistic, inquisitive, and confident. Millennials have been the subject of extensive writing, but Gen Z has received much less attention. More specifically, in terms of their perspective, motivations, and values.

However, to understand the purchasing potential and employability of Generation Z, brands and human resources firms have had to conduct extensive research on them.

Despite their aptitude for business and labor, it's critical that the parents, educators, and other stakeholders involved in the development of this generation comprehend them in order to better prepare them for work and life.

These breeds' development depends on how the family fulfills its vital role in their growth and development since the family is their initial point of contact.

Since all humans are social creatures, social structure has a significant impact on how we develop.

A child's family is the first social group with whom he or she may interact. It is the first social interaction that occurs in a baby's existence.

So, what function does a family serve in the growth of a Gen Z person?

As the first few individuals a child interacts with, the importance of the family in a child's socialization cannot be overstated. These encounters may aid a child in developing a better awareness of both himself and the people around him.

The opportunity for a child to grow more in life is provided by the way they are loved, cared for, and nurtured at home. The influence of a family on a child's growth is comparable to a foundation that can assist in molding a child's future.

A family may affect a child's development in the following ways:

Values

A child is like a sponge, soaking in all he sees or hears. Due to the possibility that the child might eventually learn from the parents, this places a great deal of duty on the parents. As a result, if you value a particular group in society or give some people more preference than others, your child may form opinions in a similar way.

Your child might be witnessing your disrespectful behavior when you interact with others. Leading by example is the most effective way to teach a child because, rather than preaching, your child is more likely to imitate what you are doing.

Additionally, it would be wise to begin instilling moral principles in children at a young age. Many people think that a young child won't be able to understand or appreciate the value of learning good values, but that might not be the case.

When you force children to comprehend the effects of their actions, they comprehend better. Assist them in comprehending the potential repercussions of their conduct. It is crucial for a family to instill good values in their children.

Social Development And Socialization

Your baby's first social group is his or her family. This implies that your child may be learning something by watching the family members. It has been found that happy families or families who treat one another with love and respect help to foster a positive view of a family for the children and set an exemplary model for social interaction.

Healthy social development may be promoted if your family spends quality time together by sharing meals, watching television, or engaging in other activities.

Additionally, the way you interact with your child aids in his learning about how to interact with others.

A child may gain a better understanding of relationships by watching how his or her family interacts with them. Only with the help of his own family can he learn to relax, make friends, and trust others. Human survival depends heavily on relationships, and a child may learn how to establish and maintain relationships from his family. The building blocks of good social skills are established at home, which may benefit your child's socialization as he gets older.

Development Abilities

A child's optimal growth and development depend heavily on his acquisition of a variety of developmental skills, including motor-cognitive, emotional intelligence, and language abilities. You should engage your child in a variety of physical activities to help him fine-tune his motor-cognitive skills in order to help him hone them.

Something that is easy or natural for you as an adult may be difficult for your child. Help your youngster develop his motor skills by teaching him to sit, walk, crawl, and run, among other similar physical exercises.

It's important to talk, read, sing, or partake in other language-based activities with your child to aid in language development. It has been noted that parents or other family members who speak to young children more frequently have better control over language.

The development of a child's various emotional skills is crucial, and a family is crucial to this process. A child learns about different emotions like love, compassion, sympathy, etc. from their family. Your child might not be able to express himself better emotionally due to a lack of appropriate emotional skills, which could result in him making unwise decisions in the future.

Security

Because his family is the only one who can take care of all of his basic needs, including food, clothing, and shelter, a child learns what security means from his family. A family gives a child the emotional security he might not otherwise have, in addition to meeting his basic survival needs. This is due to the possibility that when your child is outside, he may need to behave in a particular way or be social because he may be expected to act in accordance with social norms.

However, he can express himself freely at home, making it crucial to establish a safe environment there so that a child can do that.

A child who may be living in an unsafe environment and is not afraid to express himself freely may develop and grow more successfully than a child who may be living in an unsafe environment. A child's sense of security is very paramount, and it may play a role in how a child develops emotionally, physically, and cognitively.

Parental effort is necessary because raising a child is not an easy task. However, watching your child develop into a responsible, compassionate adult is an incredibly rewarding experience. To ensure that your child can be devoted to the lessons you have taught him, you need to not only instill in him good values and habits, but also create a supportive and safe environment for him.

Additionally, it's possible that perfection isn't always possible, and making mistakes is perfectly acceptable when raising children. Although parents are only human and may err, it is more crucial to admit their errors and try to make amends. Be gentle with yourself and your child. A child learns the most from their family, so make sure to make it a good one.

The Apple Doesn't Fall Far From The Tree

The truth is that the apple never falls too far from the tree, despite the Gen Zs' appearance as a brand-new generation. Despite having their own distinctive qualities, given their birth dates and the historical events that formed their generations, they share many traits with the GEN Y (i.e., the Millennials).

Having Fun Now Vs. Making Future Plans

Generation Z is more focused on the future than on enjoying the moment. Their understanding of reality prompts them to plan ahead and make preparations. Gen Y's risk-taking, responsible, and mature behavior has evolved into a more risk-averse lifestyle in Gen Z, giving the phrase "you only live once" a new meaning.

66 —————————————————

No apple falls far from its tree.
We are all a reflection of the generation that
came before us.

————————————————— 99

Stability And Safety Vs. Flexibility And Freedom

Since Gen Z was never exposed to the stability and prosperity of the 1990s, they have developed into dependable people who are careful and conscientious with their money. Because of the sluggish economy, Generation Z is looking for stability in their lives.

Gen Y values stability and is more likely to consider staying longer at the same job than Gen Z, who is searching for constant change in life to find the best way to pursue their dreams. However, the ability to adapt quickly to new social settings and technological advancements did not change. It will be interesting to see if the stability-seeking Gen Z has an impact on the sharing economy.

Secret Life Sharing Vs. Life Sharing

Gen Z has learned from Gen Y about the drawbacks of sharing their lives on social media. As a result, they choose apps like Whisper, Secret, or Snapchat to communicate and share their lives. By copying Snapchat's story feature, WhatsApp, Instagram, and even Skype have recently included the ephemerality feature. It is obvious from the popularity of that feature that Gen Z wants to be in charge of their digital environment. "Viral messages are transitioning into disappearing messages."

Authenticity Vs. Pseudo-Creativity

Gen Y is without doubt a creative generation and that can be attributed to their unconventional ways of thinking, fresh perspectives gained from traveling the world and experiencing various cultures, as well as the technological tools they have had access to since they were young. However, the resources they had at a young age included cracked versions of Movie Maker or Photoshop. The "fix-it-with-one button" photoshop available to Gen Z members on their phones is called Instagram, Snapchat, or FaceApp. They believe they are creative because of the stunning results these intuitive tools produce.

Unfortunately, they frequently put little real effort into the content they create, and they frequently have no idea what to expect when the magic button is pressed. On the one hand, there are those who take pride in their own easy labor and never learn the true beauty of mastering a skill or subject.

However, there is a lower barrier to entry for content creation (blogs, videos, music, live streaming, co-creation, etc.). Therefore, after a certain point, people will begin to delve further into the more complicated theories of their field.

This is demonstrated by popular YouTube stars who, after beginning with basic videos, have advanced studios, a team, and industry knowledge. So, there is undoubtedly a split, and it will be interesting to see how inventive the generation as a whole is. However, it should be noted that three out of every four respondents want to turn their current interest into full-time employment.

In Gen Y, a comparable split was present. There were those who watched YouTube, Hulu, and Netflix, as well as those who produced material, collaborated on projects for businesses, or even built the platforms from scratch. Nevertheless, remember that Gen Z is a diligent generation, particularly if they are aware of the causes they are supporting. On the other hand, Generation Y only puts in a lot of effort if they are clear about their goals.

Escapism

The yearning for escape is a distinctive trait of Generation Z. By using the internet, young people are said to be able to escape the emotional and mental challenges they experience in the physical world. Rapid technology advancements have created a highly complicated and fast-paced environment that is stressful for Generation Z.

Two instances of contemporary struggles are FOMO (FOMO–Fear of Missing Out) and FOLO (FOLO–Fear of Living Offline). In addition, there is pressure on the job market and in schooling. As a result, individuals replenish their dopamine stores by playing Candy Crush and other addictive games, consuming junk media like Facebook newsfeed, and posting affirmations on social media (Instagram likes).

Physical Engagement

It makes sense that society will return to valuing the physical environment and face-to-face interaction after the excess of digital and virtual connections. Face-to-face engagement is crucial. Outdoor advertisements are more important to 68 percent of Gen Z and to 14 percent of this generation.

DIY Instruction

Parents of Generation Y enlighten their children on how completing college is important to succeeding. Gen Z is more likely to "blend free Ivy League school classes with real world education" to further their education as opposed to relying on the conventional system, which frequently leaves students with large debt loads.

Celebrity-Oriented

Gen Z is more attracted to advertisements with athletes and celebrities than Gen Y. Additionally, Gen Zers may be able to have a closer relationship with celebrities because of social media apps like Twitter, Smule, and Snapchat.

Generation Z's Frontiers

World-Impact

Gen Z is really much more likely to have an impact on the world than Gen Y, as seen by the change in their motto from "it's not worth it" to "you have to earn it." Compared to Millennials, who only desire to change the world to a lesser extent (39%), Gen Z is 55% more likely to desire to launch a business.

Attention-Seeking

According to experts, an overprotective parenting style may be to blame for the increased craving for attention among Gen Z. Their use of social media to find affirmations can be seen as a reflection of this behavior. The young people there upload "optimized" photos, incredibly intriguing inquiries, or pointless situation updates in an effort to attract attention and feedback. In Generation Z, the desire for attention has grown.

Pre-Demand Vs. On-Demand

Both digital generations were raised with a lack of patience since they never really learnt to wait. Gen Z expects to be supplied with predictive services, whereas Gen Y was the first generation to receive information, entertainment, and tangible goods on demand via services like Google, Netflix, or Amazon Prime. They want a service to monitor the internet and alert them as soon as it comes across stuff that they find interesting. Before they ever ask for it, they anticipate that services like Periscope will gather live video from a location.

In the near future, customers might expect Amazon to estimate their product usage based on waste analysis and give them the items they would be lacking in advance. Because of the increased demand, they anticipate that services will run continuously.

Feedback Junkie: Quick Satisfaction

Because of the parenting they experienced as children, Gen Y demands immediate feedback for all of their behaviors. They were becoming more and more at ease receiving praise and comments for their deeds. Gen Z nowadays genuinely demands immediate gratification. Every action they perform should be rewarded. Examining how businesses utilize Facebook to their advantage illustrates this ambition. They always respond to comments, thank their fans, and show them appreciation.

The Need To Stay Updated

Due to the rapid pace of technological advancement, Gen Z has already made a point of focusing on innovative items and keeping up with the most recent developments. Being current is much more important to Gen Z because they experience breaking-news innovation every day as children.

It makes sense that new iPhones are sold so quickly each year and that there isn't any mention of requiring OS updates from their end. Due to their already high expectations, they do not, however, welcome every new product upgrade with enthusiasm. In this context, the term "up-to-date" can relate both to news and products.

A Short Attention Span Vs. None

It has long been established that Gen Y has a shorter attention span. This can be explained in two ways: on the one hand, by the tendency to get bored easily; and on the other, by having to deal with more information. As a result, it has been necessary to cut down on the amount of time spent on one piece of content.

The attention span of Generation Z has further shrunk due to the exponential growth in available content. Several sites mention 8 seconds. The emergence of short-form junk-food media is evidence that Gen Z members are micro-miners who require every bit of information to be broken down into smaller parts. Another example is the acceptance of Snapchat and Emoji as quick forms of visual communication. The short attention span was addressed with the app Vine, which only supported videos of six seconds. Nowadays, personalized content is essential since it pre-screens information for the user.

Experts Vs. Tech-Savvy

The fact that Gen Z was raised using technology in the

classroom and had Photoshop on their phones made them tech gurus. They make an effort to stay current, which helps with this. In comparison to older coworkers and even their superiors, Generation Z has a significant edge at work and can assist their parents with technological challenges.

This characteristic is noteworthy since Gen Z has a variety of ways to learn about a subject or, for example, a brand's reputation. Using forums, social media, and review websites like Yelp and Trip Advisor will make this simple to accomplish.

Different Viewpoints Vs. Different Identities

Gen Y was already recognized for blending different ideologies. Examples of this include feminists who practice strict religious feminism and gun-toting vegans. However, Gen Y was able to combine their various viewpoints into a single identity that they would maintain throughout all of their social media platforms.

By assuming many identities, Gen Z navigates the complexities of life and the tension between having liberal values and conventional ones. They coordinate their visuals across many social media platforms. Facebook and LinkedIn reveal their candid sides, while Instagram shows off their sophisticated side. Each identity has its own unique collection of values. Additionally, they have the capacity to instantly alter an image.

The Global Generation Against Global Interest Groups

The kids of today are more likely to travel the world through exchange programs and long-distance vacations, in addition to being globally linked via the internet. As a result, geographical boundaries are no longer an issue for today's social clusters. Peer groups are formed all around the world and are recognized by shared interests.

Young people seem to feel more and more connected to international interest groups. Smule, for instance, displays the locations of the individuals you sing with on a map of the world. For Gen Z, YouTube is the most popular platform because it allows them to easily generate content and stay informed, as well as because it connects them to people across the world and to peers who share their skills and interests.

Togetherness Vs. Tolerance

Gen Z is the most ethnically diverse generation to date in the US and was raised as a genuinely global generation. They are not the generation to discuss racial equality internally in opposition to authoritarian viewpoints. They firmly believe that individuals of different races and beliefs may coexist in society. The old gender binary and linear notions of sexuality are likewise less important to Generation Z. This is a product of particular parenting practices and instructional strategies as well. Gen Zers are globally connected and are aware of the advantages of interacting with individuals from different cultures and are committed to working together.

Gen X And Gen Y Share Common Ground

Self-Expression

Gen Y and Gen Z's primary priority is to live a life that makes them happy. They are aiming towards the top of Maslow's hierarchy of needs. People respect others most when they have freedom, which in this context is described as the ability to live the life you were created for. The status symbols of Generation Y have been freedom and self-expression rather than material success and social standing.

The Benz, or Bentley of today's youth are exclusive locales promoted by location-tags, stunning photographs of exotic food, and travel blogs about beautiful countries. Gen Z's addiction to viewing new places is so fascinating. Features like Snapchat's location-based filters allow Gen Z users to boast about the exclusive locales they are visiting because freedom and self-expression are absolutely appealing to this generation. In her song Royals, Lorde makes a powerful statement: Even though Gen Z is motivated by values other than money, and despise what the Cadillac represents. They enjoy the luxury these pricey items provide.

Being Distinct

For Generation Z, accepting variance as the foundation of uniqueness is crucial. Their parents taught them that they are unique and lovely in their own way, just like Gen Y. They do, however, assist themselves in becoming more distinctive. Still, wearing distinctive attire is one way to accomplish this.

Here's a little paradox that the mature, realistic youth who seek authenticity and reality exemplify; according to a survey, Gen Z still cares about appearance. They would rather be regarded more exceptional than authentic. They anticipate that brands will value their individuality.

Open-Minded

This phrase refers to accepting and even embracing differences. Racial equality is only one aspect of tolerance; it also includes acceptance of and lack of judgment towards all types of differences. Responses to this include campaigns like Dove Real Beauty, which support body positivity.

Being open-minded also means thinking freely and appreciating fresh perspectives. It means embracing the unknown. Gen Z views travel as a method to actively engage with various worldviews and maintain an open mind.

Snapchat frequently releases specific regional location-based filters or lenses, like the Beijing lens, which turns you into a Chinese toy, to appeal to Gen Z's curiosity about foreign cultures. The discovery feature also serves as a window into the diversity of our globe.

Connected

Finally, generations Y and Z are always connected and reachable. Gen Zs spend over 3 hours on their computers for non-school work related activities. 25% of them are online after the first five minutes of waking up, and 13-year-olds check their social media on average 100 times every day.

The 21st century's currencies are loyalty and attention, yet gaining either of them requires a thorough understanding of society. Gen Z has seen a significant shift in favor of valuing consistency, security, and more conventional types of success. However, we continue to hear the same demand for self-expression and global good just as Gen Y advocated for.

Openness, taking a practical approach to achieving their goals, and special technical expertise are unquestionably positive traits of Gen Z that other generations can learn from.

High demands, a shortened attention span, and escapism are the outcomes of the drawbacks of technology and overly concerned parenting.

It's important to keep a watch on Gen Z's degree of innovation, which benefits from lower entrance barriers but flounders owing to technology's ease of use. From realists to optimists, and with the key generation battling the conflict between liberal and traditional beliefs, the world may change.

CHAPTER THREE
Gen Z: The Digital Breed

The most recent generation's children are actually growing up in the digital era. There will never be a time when the Internet will not be available to them, and people will never be without computers and smartphones.

The Gen Z are special breeds that have come upon a world of easy internet access. That's why members of generation Z are referred to as special people because they were born in a world where the Internet had already been invented and our corded telephones had been largely replaced by smartphones. For these people, life has always been digitized. Since they were young, laptops, smartphones, and Wi-Fi have been a big part of their lives.

We have seen the challenges of growing up in the digital era and how it affects the lives of our Gen Z. However, we already see the effects it has. It's becoming clear as Gen Z enters the workforce that these "digital natives"—who are incredibly accustomed to technology—have a lot to offer.

They were raised in the digital era. What will this digital age eventually imply for them, in terms of their professional aspirations, personal lives, and social implications?

> "
> *Young people today frequently plan their occupations based solely on the advancements of the previous several decades.*
> "

A Generation Z Perspective

What distinguishes each unique generation?

The contrasts between Baby Boomers, the Silent Generation, and Millennials, to mention a few, are reflected in the influence of significant events, cultural standards, social norms, and even politics.

The impact of technology may be what sets apart our current generation of young people, known as Generation Z.

Everything changes because our children and grandchildren will never experience a world without the effectiveness and pervasiveness of technology. This indicates that the worlds of Generation Z and the worlds we knew in our youth are clearly different (and even Millennials). Future societal norms regarding how people will live and work will change as a result of the development of Internet technology. From the start, these young people have taken a very different path than previous generations.

Numerous Job Opportunities Are Available

Technology is pervasive in today's environment, and it significantly impacts the direction of business and growth. It's beyond Gen Z just being tech-aware. Generation Z is developing the skills necessary for their specific future as technology has such a significant impact on almost every industry.

At the same time, technology is expanding access to educational opportunities. Young people today frequently plan their careers based on the advancements of the previous several decades. This is undoubtedly a noticeable transition in the workplace from the manual labor jobs of the mid-20th century as well as other professions that were non-digital.

A Change In Lifestyle Goals

The lifestyle choices that Generation Z selects will undoubtedly be influenced by new career roles, in-demand work skills, and the opportunity to launch an internet business. Those who were born earlier in the 1900s had a higher likelihood of adhering to "traditional" family structures and gender norms, but technology has reversed that.

More women than ever before are employed, and many teenage girls are especially keen on pursuing professions in STEM fields. Millennials and older Gen Zs are putting off getting married and having kids so they can focus on building their own business empires. This is because there are so many ways to have a successful career in the modern world. In fact, research found that 55% of Gen Z's want to launch their own company.

> *Technology has changed the landscape of every area and industry, in addition to making us more innovative and connected.*

Various Perspectives On Technology

The enormous gap in how young people view technology is frequently what stands out to us as the older generation. There's still something essentially amazing about modern technology for people who can recall their first television.

Mobile phones, the Internet, and smart technologies are seen with much more indifference by Gen Z and even Millennials. They should not be surprised by these aspects because they are a natural part of life.

This can be perceived as depressing in some aspects.

Does Generation Z lose that sense of wonder?

Will they ever understand just how amazing today's technology is?

These, however, are only sentimental ideas. Instead, Gen Z and Millennials just respond to current technology differently, and this will only aid them in the future. Kids won't be concerned despite the exponential growth of technology. The next step can seem even more feasible because these digital leaps don't seem as astounding. Maybe that positivity will help our upcoming generation of scientists, engineers, and developers.

Even the most cutting-edge technology is incredibly comfortable and familiar to Generation Z.

No More Distance

Speaking of optimism, there is a perception that things are always within the grasp of Generation Z. After all, children have grown up in a world where quick news updates from around the world are commonplace, real-time video conferencing with friends and family is possible from anywhere, and the Internet has made the world seem much smaller.

Gen Z is therefore likely to have a strong sense of drive and self-assurance as they get older. They have the conviction that they can achieve their goals easily since technology will make it possible.

They Exist In An Efficient World

The Internet has altered how we interact with others, fall in love, look for employment, arrange our vacations, and much more. Is there any part of modern life that the Internet hasn't impacted?

Ultimately, efficiency is what makes a significant impact in each of these areas. Thanks to the Internet, nearly everything can now be done more quickly and effectively. Gen Zers are digital natives who have grown up in this incredibly efficient society, and this has undoubtedly had an impact on their lives.

A Capacity For Adaptation

Older people are frequently criticized for being "stuck in their ways" or resistant to embracing cutting-edge technology. This might be partially true. However, it is much more of an "ask" for folks who have spent most of their lives without the convenience of having smartphones close at hand.

Technology changes and adaptation is at a breakneck pace, and Generation Z (and perhaps especially Millennials) have seen all of these variations. This has probably produced a generation that is highly flexible and adaptive and knows how to roll with the punches.

It's not difficult to envision that this trait will benefit the younger generations as they mature, since it is advantageous in both one's personal and professional life. Even now, AI is establishing itself, and smart devices are becoming more widely used. Young people will continue to absorb new technology as they get older and become adults because they are already acclimated to these space-age technologies.

At least half of Gen Xers, Millennials, and Gen Zers report appreciating the ability of AI to recommend goods and services.

Digital Challenges To Combat

Of course, not all aspects of our constantly connected environment are advantageous. There are a few areas where Gen Zers may have to experience difficulties. After all, technology cannot prepare a person for everything in life! Here are a few difficulties that might be inherent in a person's digital existence;

Having To Put Imagination First

We used to play with paper dolls and real action figures back then. But now, there is no doubt that the presence of screens in their hands has decreased the amount of time they spend engaging in non-digital, imaginative play.

This presents a special challenge to Gen Z, who must consciously make an effort to prioritize spending time using their imagination and creativity. When a child is young, parents can assist by restricting screen time and promoting outdoor activities, but as the child grows into an adult, it becomes his duty.

The Gen Z or Millennial will need to set aside time to unplug from their electronics in order to grow up to be a healthy and well-rounded adult. They will need to set aside time to concentrate on their artistic and creative endeavors. For their own well-being, they will also need to learn to manage their screen time responsibly.

> *One could be deemed an internet addict if they develop a mental illness and show signs of mental instability as a result of engaging in online gambling, online bidding, adult websites, and other web activities.*

More Work Is Needed To Develop Social Skills

In recent years, there has been considerable worry that Gen Z's reliance on the Internet and social media is impairing their capacity for social interaction. They might not learn the crucial social skills required for face-to-face engagement because they frequently rely on technology as their main means of communication with others.

Technology encourages users to become accustomed to communicating via screens and to choose texting or emailing over calling. Unfortunately, text-only conversations lose a lot of context and significance. Some would argue that the younger generations are losing their ability to communicate.

Of course, over the past ten years, there has also been an increase in cyberbullying. Children don't need new ways to encounter bullying throughout the difficult adolescent years, but social media and smartphone apps have sadly made this a reality.

Likewise, as this problem is becoming more widely known, organizations and schools are taking proactive measures to put a stop to cyberbullying. While there may be some unsettling parts for children growing up in the digital age, it appears that they will learn how to confront these issues.

Specific Concerns For Safety And Security

When it comes to our online data, today's digital natives (as well as us grownups) have to cope with a variety of privacy concerns.

It makes sense that parents worry that if their kids disclose too much information online, it could compromise their safety or violate their privacy. We might not need to worry as much as we think, though. The younger generations have found a way to use the privacy settings on their social media accounts more effectively, and they are gradually learning to be more conscious of privacy issues.

Because they are accustomed to using several platforms, they could feel more at ease changing these settings. However, it appears that Generation Z favors more private social media sites, particularly ones that give you strict control over who you engage with, like Instagram and Snapchat. These young people are leaving Facebook, which appears to be the website most prone to privacy issues.

Generation Z is most likely to be aware of the risks associated with lax online security. However, they are also the group that is most adept at distinguishing between their everyday and online selves.

They Have Trouble Unwinding And Letting Go

Members of Generation Z may experience overstimulation as a result of their continual screen engagement because they are digital natives. There are already a lot of us (including teenagers) who acknowledge that we use our devices excessively, and there is abundant proof that this screen addiction causes tension and worry.

Gen Z excels at multitasking and may even feel as though they are not performing well if they are not actively multitasking.

This skill has some clear advantages, but it can also quickly result in overstimulation. When the brain doesn't get a chance to relax, burnout happens considerably more quickly.

Employers might make "digital detox" a requirement in a few years. It will be up to these young adults to determine how to strike the right balance between work and life in the technologically advanced future.

The Magic Of A Digital World

In the end, people who were raised in the digital age have it good in a variety of ways.

We cannot ignore the many paths to success or the ways in which technology has significantly enhanced the world for our children and for future generations, even though some sacrifices might need to be made.

Technology has changed the landscape of every area and industry, in addition to making us more innovative and connected. Modern technology is saving lives in fields like medicine.

The next generation may be quite fortunate. They might anticipate ongoing medical advancements and discoveries that may result in disease cures or elimination, as well as a longer life expectancy.

As Gen Z ages, ameliorative care will contribute to a higher level of health and wellbeing.

Additionally, this generation has extraordinary awareness. In the last few decades, environmental risks and other possible bad effects have become a bigger worry.

However, because they were exposed to so many warnings as children, it's possible that Generation Z may take the lead and implement the required changes. This entails emphasizing sustainable lifestyles and moving along the proper environmental path.

The New Addictions

There's no doubt that technology has made it easier for Gen Z to connect with people all over the world. This comes with a host of new costs and causes their parents and guardians a great deal of worry.

Every parent's worst dread is the discovery that one of their children has a substance addiction. Addiction in teenagers can take many different forms. The detrimental impacts of drug and alcohol addiction on youngsters' lives have already been discussed with parents.

Parents must realize that addiction in children does not just develop through drug and alcohol use. Teenagers are developing addictions to a variety of things. The majority of these addictions are a result of developments in modern culture and the digital age.

Texting

One of the most remarkable outcomes of modern technology is the creation of cellphones, which allow users to make and receive calls and text messages whenever they choose. However, texting is a mode of communication that has turned into a risky preoccupation for many people, especially Generation Z. One can see people clutching their phones and texting everywhere, from the streets to the stores. Some people are unable to even go one minute without checking their phones.

Despite appearing harmless, texting can have a significant negative impact on the lives of Gen Z. They are unable to complete key tasks like their schoolwork and lesson preparation because of it. Additionally, texting has an impact on how people handle their social and personal lives. Some people are even inclined to send texts while driving as a result of this addiction.

Setting limits on cellphone use while at home is one thing parents may do to fight this addiction. If at all possible, parents should take away their children's phones when they are eating and completing homework. It is best if they inform their kids about the negative effects of constant texting.

Using Social Networks

Numerous social media platforms, including Twitter, Facebook, Instagram, and TikTok, are being used by more and more people. Teenagers devote a large portion of their daily time to updating their accounts. Some people already incorporate monitoring these social networking sites into their everyday routines.

The manner in which Gen Z interacts with others and communicates has changed as a result of the use of social networking. Due to the fact that students spend more time on these social websites than studying, it also impacts their academic achievement. According to a study, using social media for more than three hours a day is linked to unhealthy Gen Z behaviors like drinking, smoking, and engaging in sexual activity.

The easiest method to avoid this kind of addiction in kids is to set limits on how much time they spend online. Parents need to make sure that their kids abide by the restrictions placed on internet use. When necessary, parents can block access to numerous social networking sites on their browser to ensure that their kids' online interactions are kept to a minimum. It would be beneficial if they encouraged their kids to contact them in person rather than through social media.

Numerous people's lives are improved by social networking sites. But excessive use of these websites can have negative effects as well. Teenagers ought to be mature enough to understand how to use these websites appropriately.

The Internet Addict

Who exactly qualifies as an internet addict? Is anyone who uses the internet frequently considered one? Of course not; it would be absurd to categorize as an internet addict everybody who logs on frequently.

There are numerous good reasons to use the internet for both business and leisure. For anything to become an addiction, a person would need to have an unquenchable and insatiable need for it. Investigating what causes addiction is fascinating!

What Constitutes An Addiction?

At what point does someone become an addict? Well, many professionals in the area agree that internet addiction occurs when a person is dependent on a feature of the internet. One could be deemed an internet addict if they develop an illness and show signs of mental instability as a result of engaging in online gambling, online bidding, adult websites, and other web activities.

When they are unable to access these sites, those who are addicted to or emotionally dependent on them become agitated and restless. While spending many hours on these sites, many have been observed to lose consciousness of their identities.

What potential immediate and long-term repercussions can these victims experience?

Internet Addiction's Effects

As with any other addiction, being addicted to the internet can make people act in strange ways, and certain patterns often appear. Given that many people spend a lot of time online at night, one of the most frequent results is a diminished capacity to operate regularly during the day.

According to some experts in the field, cutting off internet access can cause extreme anxiety and other withdrawal symptoms, just like with other addictions.

Internet addiction is unmistakably a phenomenon that is still developing but is already gaining ground. Can we halt or stop the spread of another mental illness that we seem to have produced on our own? Or will it eventually lead to the next major disturbance in our lives and the lives of our loved ones? I suppose that with the little knowledge we may have learned here, we may be able to recognize potential victims and even assist some before it is too late.

"You Caused It." Gen Z to Gen Y

Smartphone addiction is a contentious topic in many households. If you say that you have not discussed the significant "screen problem" facing Gen Z, you would be lying.

But despite the accusing finger being pointed in their direction and our inability to comprehend the "youth of today," some people think their instructors and parents played a role in the new addiction that they are all struggling with.

Some time ago, Audrey's parents brought her to me for a session. They believed their daughter had an addiction to her gadgets. During our session, Audrey shared her opinion on the issue with me. She stated how her parents have been bombarding her with gadgets since she was a kid. She also explained how her teachers encouraged them to do research on their gadgets. In obeying her parents and teachers, she got addicted to being with her phone. She was just dazed at how her parents were claiming she was addicted to using her phone.

Her brother Daniel seemed to share the same thought. He sent me an email as a response to the message I left him about his parents requesting that I have a session with him.

"It's out of control how much time we spend on our phones. I can now see how big of a deal this is. However, it would be unfair to attribute this issue to simply my generation. I believe that our parents and instructors should have a significant share of the blame for the fact that many of us are addicted.

I'm getting pretty sick of my parents and teachers complaining about how much my friends and I use our phones. However, we wouldn't be in such a big mess if the adults had established limits at home and at school in the first place. If there were rules established from the start, I can assure you that there would be considerably fewer of us who were addicted.

My generation has a phone addiction that affects more than half of the population. But it's not always our fault. When these new technologies were developed, our parents didn't impose restrictions and didn't consider how addicting the gadgets would become.

You can categorically say that we are all addicts.

I'll admit that I have a phone addiction, but that's because neither my parents nor my teachers ever set up adequate boundaries. It has been considerably tougher for me to kick my addiction because, up until pretty much this year, I've always lived in a setting where using a phone while sitting down was acceptable. It would have been simpler if my dependence on my phone had never developed.

I would strongly advise it if you were thinking about getting your kid a phone. Just make sure to set very firm boundaries and rules in this area, and don't let your children talk you out of them. To confirm that the regulations are being followed, speak with the instructors or administrators at your child's school.

For myself, my recent digital detox has truly demonstrated to me how much can be accomplished in the time I might otherwise spend mindlessly scrolling through pointless social media.

My awareness of how much I actually use my phone has been greatly increased. Even parents should practice digital detox, in my opinion."

According to recent scientific findings, smartphone addicts exhibit the same symptoms as drug addicts. The same can happen to actual "smartphone addicts," much like some drug users might become so dependent that it strains their personal, social, and professional lives.

They can find themselves putting off chores, time with the kids, and other obligations so they can check their Facebook page or play a little more Clash of Clans.

How come there aren't rules addressing something just as addicting as Internet addiction consuming the lives of children, if there are regulations for addictive items like drugs or alcohol?

Mobile phones are increasingly being given to children at such young ages. Children as young as 12, 11, or 10 are getting their first phones. And after a short while, these "tweens" develop addictions.

But their parents are also to blame for it. Parents wait too long to establish limits, which allows their kids to become dependent on their phones as a crutch. It wouldn't start World War III if there was a thirty-minute time limit on screens for children as discipline for misbehavior.

School is the same way. Many students at my school are opposed to the idea of a phone ban, which is being discussed by the teachers. There wouldn't be a huge dispute between the students and staff over what to do if there were guidelines or time restrictions in place from the first day phones were allowed in the classroom.

Myths Surrounding Generation Z

Earlier this year, a member of Generation Z, was asked to participate as a guest speaker at a youth conference about common misconceptions about his generation.

Here are some of his observations:

We are starting to see the biases and preconceptions of our generation as the spotlight moves from Millennials to Generation Z. While some portray us as a digitally adept group of people, many are a little off the mark.

As a member of Gen Z, I've chosen a few "facts," or perhaps more appropriately, myths, about my generation to explore in greater detail.

Myth #1: We favor electronic communication over in-person interaction.

Although I believe that this age is totally engrossed in mobile technology, this is not just done to avoid social connection. Gen Z enjoys the advantages of being able to stay in touch with their friends and loved ones online while still thriving on interpersonal engagement.

These days, music festivals are becoming increasingly popular, and lawn seats at concerts are selling out more quickly than normal seats. All of these promote networking and socializing and permit more private time with friends.

Myth #2: We are too young to make an impact.

Although the exact dates aren't known, Gen Z roughly spans the mid-1990s to the mid-2000s, with the oldest being around 25 at the moment. At this age, people start working and becoming young professionals. We should be the focus of your research and instruction because we are young professionals. We're known for our eagerness to contribute and learn new things.

We don't just concentrate on our own goals; rather, we consider how we might change the world. Take advantage of that and provide us with the knowledge we require to guide the future ("team player" and "selflessness" are not traits I would consider negative.

Myth #3: Because we have short attention spans, we are difficult to entertain. When you Google "Gen Z," the phrase "8-second attention span" comes up immediately. I won't argue that this statistic is unreliable. Although we do have short attention spans, this is because we prioritize our tasks more than other people.

As I've already said, we prioritize having a lasting influence and experiencing life to the fullest. We commit our time to important tasks, which may require more time and investigation on the part of association management.

CHAPTER FOUR
Gen Z: The Highly Connected

As Generation Z leaves their parents' homes, attends college, and begins their careers, technology is an ever-present component of their lives. In spite of the fact that technology is all around them, we need to concentrate on making the most of its potential while reducing the amount of abuse it causes. Some of the vices they engaged in when they were younger might no longer be tolerated as they get older.

In order for young digital natives to develop in a well-polished manner, parents and other stakeholders must be aware of how to effectively guide them to make the most of the advantages they have over previous generations.

The ability of members of Generation Z to connect with people who live in different parts of the world is one of the generation's greatest strengths.

Not all Gen Z are addicts or victims who are just at the mercy of modern technology. They come from different backgrounds and have a vast variety of different interests when it comes to the topic of technology. Even though they have a technological advantage over older generations, they still need to be taught how to connect the dots in order for them to reach their full potential.

My Take On The Digital World

There have been countless technological triumphs throughout the history of mankind, each of which has brought us into a new age by virtue of the innovations they have brought. Things such as the Industrial Revolution, the Automobile Age, and the Introduction of Electricity have fundamentally altered the way in which we live our lives, and they will continue to have significant and far-reaching effects over the next millennium.

However, despite all of our wonderful achievements, there is one thing that stands out from the others and is likely to be regarded as the most significant turning point in our civilization. I am sure that you are already aware of the significant technological development that is the internet. The Internet is bringing about rapid change in the way we live our lives since it has the ability to provide endless and painless contact throughout the globe.

Regardless of whether you consider yourself a "digital immigrant" or a "digital nomad," the effects of having a worldwide and collaborative interconnected network have undoubtedly had some kind of impact on you. You have been impacted in some ways, whether it is in your daily commute, as light signals on roadways or just in how you pay for your morning coffee at Starbucks.

Products and services are being improved all around the world so that they are compatible with the internet and the "digital society."

Someone who has grown up around technology and has always had it easily available is said to be a "digital native." As a result of my upbringing, I've got the chance to make the most of the internet and take advantage of all of its features.

The phrase "simply Google it" serves as the response to a great number of the inquiries that I receive on a daily basis. My personal development in terms of socialization has also been significantly influenced by the internet. My sense of self has become so entwined with the internet to the point where I have no idea who I would be if I had been born one hundred years earlier.

Many individuals believe that this is contributing to our culture as a whole. Being significantly more sedentary and less physically active is another thing that is said about us. This remark may have some truth to it, but it does not take into account all of the positive outcomes that might result from encounters of this kind.

For instance, what begins with instant messaging (IM) with your friends can lead to a better and easier communication channel that will be with you for the rest of your life and can help you in the "real world" of corporate America.

This process is known as "anticipatory socialization," and it can help you. This is a talent and an attribute that no one should ever take for granted.

Living in a culture that is increasingly dependent on technology has better prepared me for a future in which more and more of the jobs we perform will be performed by computers or optimized to function more smoothly.

People no longer produce their papers using typewriters as they used to, and as we progress further into the future, it is difficult to predict what it will have in store for us.

The manifest functions of the Internet are becoming more and more obvious on a daily basis, but the latent functions of the Internet are where our attention should really be focused. If you are old enough to be reading this, then the future does not lie with you; it lies with your children.

As new technologies are introduced at almost the speed of light from all corners of the globe, parents need to focus on what the long-term effects of such a digital society may have on their children.

Connected For The Better

In spite of its dangers, children can benefit from using social media by taking advantage of the many opportunities it provides to build their skills and leave a positive digital footprint. Parents should talk to their children about these and other advantages of using social media so they can get the most out of it.

It is essential to have a solid understanding of the benefits that can be gained from using social media so that you can provide your child with the direction they require to get the most out of their time.

"

Despite the fact that technology is all around, we need to concentrate on making the most of its potential while reducing the amount of abuse it causes.

"

The Benefits Of Collaborative Learning

Gen Z can gain a deeper understanding of the world around them and expand their knowledge on a variety of subjects by gaining exposure to and developing an appreciation for a variety of viewpoints and worldviews. They are able to discover areas of interest and use the platforms in an educational capacity as a result of the large number of ideas that are shared across the platforms.

Development Of Communication And Technical Skills

While gaining knowledge of digital media, it is important for the young to learn how to communicate online because social media is now a part of everyday life. This will prepare them for future employment chances and improve their relationships with friends and family.

Positive Effects On Mental Health And Wellbeing

Meeting new people, keeping in touch with old ones, and forging connections across national boundaries are all made easier thanks to social media. It is a great way for those with disabilities or those who may not feel they can connect with others within their community to connect with other people who share their ideas and interests.

An Avenue For Support

It can open up opportunities to offer support to friends and family that may be experiencing a particular challenge. On the other hand, for some young people, it might be a location where they can seek assistance if they are experiencing something they cannot discuss with their loved ones.

Campaigning For Social Causes

Young individuals who are passionate about a cause and want to make a difference in the real world can get help from social media platforms in generating awareness about that cause.

Develop A Positive Digital Footprint

Gen Z can also utilize their accounts as personalized CVs to share their achievements, showcase their talents, and build a positive online portfolio that will assist them later in life.

Be An Excellent Role Model

Set an example for the kind of conduct you want them to exhibit on their various social media platforms. Children and teenagers have a tendency to mimic the actions of adults, so it is essential to model the same morals and ethics that you would like them to embrace.

Promote Social Good

Find ways for them to use their social media following for good, such as advocating for a cause that will benefit others or sharing content that will provide support and positively impact their digital footprint. Consider how their social media following can be used for good, and give them access to the necessary resources.

Provide Them With The Appropriate Resources

Make sure that teenagers are aware of how to make use of the privacy settings offered by social media platforms so that they may maintain control over who they share information with, when they share it, and what content from other users' accounts shows up on their accounts.

Keep Up With Your Social Obligations

Actively search for opportunities to talk to people about what they post on social media, who they share with, and how the content they see on their social feed is affecting them so that you may provide help at the appropriate time for them.

The phrase "finding the correct balance" comes to mind. In order to prevent them from becoming overly dependent on the approval and opinions of interactions that are solely conducted online, which may have a detrimental effect on them, you should encourage them to build strong real-life relationships outside of social media.

PART TWO

CHAPTER FIVE
Relationship:
Through The Lens Of A Gen Z

Gen Z, also known as iGen, is the first generation to be so outspoken and brazen about opposing norms and lacking excitement to follow the order of finding love, getting married, and having babies. As a whole, Gen Z is the generation that has the most laid-back attitude toward the key life events of having children or getting married, despite the fact that there are members of previous generations who have made the decision not to have children or get married.

They like to test the waters and weigh their options well before settling down, and in some cases, even after settling down, while they are still earning financial freedom, so they are not quick to commit because of this.

Despite the fact that numerous studies and research have demonstrated that members of Generation Z do not place a high value on marriage, one thing has become abundantly clear: these individuals are concerned with love, profound connections, and discovering who they are.

Aside from studies and research, this generation has also shown that they would rather wait until they are financially independent before walking down the aisle.

They are not self-centered in any way or form, despite the fact that they focus almost entirely on themselves. They are aware that they are the ones responsible for their own success and happiness, and they understand that in order to be able to care for others, they must first be able to care for themselves. Therefore, they are not delaying long-term partnerships because they do not want them; rather, they are doing it because they require more time to establish themselves as individuals first.

> **"**
> *This generation would rather wait until they are financially independent before walking down the aisle.*
> **"**

Generation Z places a high priority on achieving financial autonomy; as a result, the aspiration to free themselves from monetary constraints is widespread within this group, which in turn influences how, when, and where they look for romantic partners as well as how they manage their personal finances.

For example, it is customary for the bride's parents to pay for the wedding; yet, research conducted on Generation Z reveals that around one third of this age group intends to pay for their own wedding. Despite the fact that this will necessitate the creation of a stringent wedding budget, it is more evidence that members of Generation Z have a strong desire to be financially independent and secure.

When asked in what sequence they would desire events to occur in their life, 79% of members of Generation Z, according to a study, stated that they would like to achieve financial stability and independence before getting married and having children. More than half of members of Gen Z aim to be their own boss and build up several streams of income in the hopes of exercising greater control over their finances and having lower levels of debt. This comes as no surprise.

Still, they desire a wedding.

Although the amassing of wealth is important to Gen Z, a sizable portion of this generation still hopes to tie the knot at some point in their lives and raise their offspring in two-parent households with both sets of grandparents. They have reached a point in their lives where getting married is no longer the central focus.

They are brave enough to see the long-standing issues that have persisted within the organization and are committed to working toward a solution, albeit one that is unique to them. Before they ever consider committing to someone for the long haul, they want to build themselves up to be well-rounded individuals who have a wealth of life experiences under their belts.

On the other hand, members of Generation Z do not look to their parents as examples of what love should be or how it should feel. Despite the fact that almost sixty percent of members of Generation Z were raised in households with two parents, many of them are skeptical about the possibility of having a similar love story.

When it comes to romantic partnerships, it appears that members of this generation have a clear idea of what they do and do not want, as well as a basic understanding of "toxic" characteristics that they are unable to overlook.

Gen Zers care more about having a deeper emotional connection with their significant other than people from previous generations. That connection includes a high level of intimacy, which is one of the most important factors in determining how long a relationship with a Gen Z person will last. Unfortunately, people of this generation display difficulties in creating connections, which are obstacles that they make for themselves.

Because Generation Z gives in to "clout culture" to such an extreme degree, the starting point for many of their romantic partnerships is the romantic pairings of other individuals and celebrities that they see online.

Their romantic connections are mainly reliant on social media platforms rather than getting to know each other on a more personal level. The development of dating apps has resulted in an increase in the number of options for meeting new people. This is an undemanding activity that can be carried out at any time.

Furthermore, 60% of Gen Zers believe that dating services allow them to meet others regardless of where they are physically located. Because some members of Gen Z are still very young, it is difficult to forecast fully how exactly these online interactions will grow over the course of time.

Communication abilities among members of Gen Z are severely lacking, which contributes to the generation's overall pessimism. People do not communicate as effectively as they used to because technology has made it more difficult for them to do so. As a result, they do not have the same kinds of connections as they did in the past.

Different people move at their own unique pace. This is perfectly normal and acceptable. However, the issue arises when people are hesitant to confess this to the people they are in committed relationships with. This results in circumstances that are highly volatile and cause discomfort on both ends.

Even though most people try to avoid making any kind of commitment, many of a couple's friends put pressure on them once they are in a committed relationship. The modern stages of adolescent romantic relationships, which move at the speed of light from zero to sixty, mark the beginning of the "talking stage."

> 66
> *It really should not come as much of a surprise to learn that members of Generation Z also use technology to look for potential romantic partners.*
> 99

What is the talking stage? You may wonder.

The talking stage, as its name suggests, isn't just talking. The talking stage is an early phase of dating in which you are still getting to know one another without a specific goal in mind. It can be regarded as the trial period of a relationship in order to determine if the two parties are compatible. You're attracted to each other, but you're unsure if you want to explore that attraction and develop a meaningful relationship. So, you are discussing matters while awaiting the outcome.

During this phase, you may go out to dinner with the individual you're speaking with. You may go home with them, spend the night, create a rapport with their pet, and leave on a friendly note. Moreover, you may still be unaware of what they are seeking or whether they even like you. It would also be inappropriate to inquire given that you are currently speaking.

At this stage, you are merely exploring the possibility of a relationship with the person you are speaking with. You are just talking to the person to see if you want to get to know them better. In addition, you may be engaged in conversation with multiple individuals. During the talking period, you have the "luxury" of having all your goals discussed without being in an official relationship. Being at this stage indicates that you are not exclusive and are not even dating.

After the talk stage comes the hangout. It's not a date.

Hanging out is usually a less formal form of the traditional going on a date. In this case, the outing is not clearly thought out or planned and the manner of asking is mostly casual—that is, you are asked that day or a few hours/minutes before the outing. It could be a night out to a bar or the movies with mutual or other friends.

Even though hangouts are fun and will help you pass the time, you should think about whether you want to do that with this person in the long run, especially if you are starting to feel something for them.

A date shows some special interest in a special person. There are no ambiguities about how they feel about you; you can tell by the way they ask, the location they choose, how they dress, how they speak to you on the outing, and so on. Unlike the hangout, where you are left to figure things out for yourself, this sends a clear message—they are interested in you.

If you like someone enough after that, suddenly you two are officially dating. Not simply dating, by the way, because for some inexplicable reason this generation has decided that "dating" and having a boyfriend or girlfriend are synonymous (they're not, for the record!).

This indicates that you are dating someone who you're loyal to and that you are about to use the "L" word any moment now. You were trying to determine their favorite song twenty minutes ago, but now you're "committed" and "loyal" to them.

Love is something that should naturally come with time, trust, and experiences you both share. It is not something you say to someone you hung out at an open bar with. However, Gen Zers do not rate it that way, such that they are quick to use the word and also withhold it as they deem fit.

On the topic of marriage:

This colorful, fluid, and socially aware generation has become known for breaking tradition. They continue to disappoint their parents by waiting longer to get married compared to previous generations, thereby raising the marital median to age 27.
It's no surprise that the age of love, marriage, and making babies is now considered an ancient way of thinking for them.

However, one thing is certain: when they do feel relationship-ready, choosing a long-term partner means finding someone who can match their own personal values (i.e., anti-racist, non-homophobic, vegetarian, and any other values they may have) and refusing to settle for less.

Due to the ever-changing nature of Gen Z that we've noticed in how they frequently change jobs, move cities, and switch up their styles, it's only natural that their relationship won't be stuck in time as well. The fluidity of this generation extends beyond pushing their marriage age but also what their identity is and unboxing the boxes.

Ultimately, Generation Z is a collection of non-committal, avaricious, independence-seeking individuals who are all eager for a rom-com love story regardless of where it can be found or what gender offers it, but not anytime soon. There is still hope for them, despite the fact that they will require a great deal of work before settling down.

Platonic

Just like romantic relationships have been "remodeled" to suit Gen Z, platonic relationships are getting a "face lift" as well, such that friendships are now viewed in a way that is different from how older generations viewed them.

Even though it seems like they shouldn't have that problem because of the advent of social media, where you can connect with the tap of a button, members of Generation Z who were born during the digital age have had some difficulty keeping up with and maintaining their friendships.

Because of the widespread availability of social media platforms in today's world, maintaining friendships shouldn't be difficult because you can stay in touch with your pals whenever it's convenient for you to do so. This is in contrast to previous generations, who did not have the luxury of having social media at their disposal.

On the other hand, research has revealed that people between the ages of 18 and 24 are more likely than people of any other age group to go more than a year without seeing their close friends. Even while members of Generation Z are more connected than ever before because of technological advancements, it's possible that their overreliance on social media is hindering their capacity to form and maintain relationships with real-life peers.

Another study found that 63% of individuals between the ages of 18 and 24 have the least amount of confidence when speaking with strangers. Additionally, it was observed that 57% of them communicated with their friends on social networking platforms more frequently than in person. It is likely that the current generation has become so acclimated to the worries associated with social media and technology that they no longer recognize them.

As many as 52% of the young people interviewed said that they considered only the people they knew from online platforms as friends.

When questioned, the vast majority of young people responded that their friends were typically the ones with whom they would communicate online.

> "
> *The act of breaking tradition is what has come to define this colorful, fluid, and socially conscious generation, as they continue to disappoint their parents by waiting longer to settle down compared to past generations.*
> "

Members of this generation tend to have the bulk of their relationships (platonic or romantic) online, and because of this, it is possible that the language of friendship and relationships needs to be reconsidered to accommodate them.

They now look to likes on Instagram, retweets on Twitter, views on Snapchat, followers on TikTok, and comments on Facebook for validation.

The fact that members of the digital generation are at greater danger of social isolation than any other group demonstrates how critical it is to maintain in-person relationships with one's friends. For the sake of cultivating friendships that will last a lifetime, young people should be encouraged to "go the distance" and see their friends in person.

However, it is not all bad news when it comes to the matter of maintaining friendships for this generation. This is the age where most of them meet their best friends.

Despite the fact that they have a lot going on and place a high priority on their existing connections, Gen Zers are looking for new friendships in order to push themselves and develop as people. Because of this, those they are interested in being friends with are typically individuals who are different from the friends they already have.

On the other hand, Millennials are looking for new connections based on new hobbies, which their previous friends may not share, as well as new friendships based on shared goals, which they can motivate and support one another in accomplishing.

CHAPTER SIX
Generation Z At Work

Just as companies were beginning to grow comfortable working with members of the millennial generation, a new generation known as Gen Z is getting ready to enter the workforce. Gen Z is now the "baby" of the labor force, and, as each generation has a custom of doing, they're disrupting things.

A job that is meaningful at a firm that makes a difference, is in alignment with their social values, and gives mental health support are all things that are important to Gen Z, but what matters most to them is a conducive working environment. They are demanding these things in a novel and audacious manner, transforming flexibility and well-being from workplace rewards to workplace standards.

For members of Gen Z, if their current employment doesn't meet those requirements, they do not hesitate to leave for a better opportunity elsewhere. This is one reason why members of this generation, along with Millennials, are leading in the Great Resignation.

The Great Resignation, also known as the Big Quit or the Great Reshuffle, refers to the continuous economic trend of more people willingly leaving their positions between late 2020 and early 2021. However, resignation data shows this pattern began more than a decade ago.

Possible causes include salary stagnation in the face of rising costs of living, long-term dissatisfaction with current employment, worries about safety brought on by the COVID-19 pandemic, and a desire to work for organizations that have more favorable policies on working from home.

However, many people are also experiencing another, less-talked-about phenomenon that is known as "shift shock," whereby they leave after starting a new job they find out that the position is not at all what they expected it to be.

> **"**
> *Gen Z is now the baby of the labor force, and, as each generation has a custom of doing, they are disrupting things.*
> **"**

Shift shock is the realization, upon starting a new job, that the position or firm is significantly different from what you had been taught to think. A survey conducted in early 2022 revealed that 72% of over 2000 respondents had experienced shift shock.

The truth is that the aspiration to have a place of employment that recognizes one's limits and requirements is ingrained generationally and this will not alter. This will get stronger with every successive generation.

Generation Z and millennial candidates, who are more inclined to believe the employer-employee relationship should be a two-way street, is driving the great resignation. In addition, the epidemic has reinforced for many that "life is short," so candidates are less inclined to remain in unsatisfying positions.

Gen Z is particularly concerned about work-life balance and personal wellness. The importance of income and brand reputation is the lowest.

Gen Z has a distinct mentality! Generation Z requires benefits such as paid time off, mental health days, and activities that foster a sense of community. Therefore, firms seeking to recruit and retain talent must examine what they can give Generation Z that promotes a healthy lifestyle and higher well-being. These questions will serve as a guide.

Is your organization rethinking standard employee benefits?

Are you developing a culture that recognizes the individual as a whole and not merely what they can accomplish in eight hours per day?

Characteristics Of Gen Z In The Workspace

Generation Z is unique in comparison to previous generations, and as a result, the priorities and standards they have for themselves are likewise distinctive. This generation, which has grown up in a period of rapid technological advancement, brings with it their very own standards and goals.

This generation saw the effects that the global recession that began in 2008 had on their families. Because of this, they have witnessed the decline of the economy. In fact, they have witnessed their parents lose their careers and their families lose their homes, in addition to witnessing their grandparents return to the workforce in order to support the family financially. Because of this, it is crucial to understand the characteristics and traits of Generation Z in order to establish an environment at work that promotes their success.

Here are a few characteristics of Gen Z in the workspace:

Generation Z In The Workplace Prefers Security And Stability

It is essential to acknowledge that Generation Z is less prone to taking chances than previous generations. This current generation will never forget the strain that came with having to grow up in an uncertain world. The massive amount of debt incurred through student loans is a major concern for Generation Z.

Because of this, they place a high value on the stability of their jobs and their finances. They are more likely to generate trust in your company if you provide them with opportunities for promotion and invest in the development of their skills. The defining characteristic of Generation Z is their incessant search for long-term stability.

Generation Z Is The Mobile-First Generation

Members of Generation Z are more accustomed to utilizing mobile devices and tablets than desktop computers. This is because Gen Z members are the first generation to have grown up in the era of mobile phones. They are the generation that is quite well-informed when it comes to using various forms of technology.

This generation is a mobile-driven workforce, whether they are researching possible employers, applying for jobs, or utilizing applications at work. Whether they are doing any of these things, they are heavily reliant on their mobile gadgets. Because of this, strategies for mobile engagement need to be put in place in order to improve the ability of Generation Z to retain information and increase their level of productivity.

To get the attention of Generation Z in the workplace, businesses need to use cutting-edge technologies and digital tools.

The Workplace Communication Of Generation Z

Generation Z was raised with mobile devices and is accustomed to texting and messaging. More than half of Gen Zers spend around 10 hours per week online, playing games, educating themselves, responding to work-related messages, managing social media, communicating with the outside world, or just for entertainment. They are entirely dependent on technology and are said to switch between three to four screens (TV, smartphone, laptop, and tablet) throughout the day.

Even though Gen Zers believe in technology, surveys show that they prefer face-to-face communication at work. They are more confident in face-to-face communication than prior generations. This could be because they find it difficult to grasp the intricacies of written communication and prefer the assurance that comes with personal engagement. In addition, they favor direct communication and face-to-face interactions with their bosses. In-person communication may occur via Google Meet, Zoom, Facetime, or any other tool.

> " ─────────────────────────
> *For members of Gen Z, if their current employment does not meet those requirements, they do not hesitate to leave for a better opportunity elsewhere.*
> ───────────────────────── "

Generation Z's Work Expectations Are Unique

The idea of digital nomads emerged as a result of the demand among members of Generation Z for flexibility and the ability to work remotely. (Digital nomads are professionals working in online and knowledge-based industries such as digital marketing, IT, design, writing, and consulting).

Actually, these two prerequisites come in at number one and number two, respectively, on the list of expectations held by Generation Z. In addition to these elements, they place a considerable emphasis on maintaining an open and honest environment within the company. They are always on the lookout for opportunities to expand their skill sets, move up in their professions, and make a more significant impact on the organizations for which they work.

Additionally, individuals of Generation Z have a great desire to make use of the most up-to-date equipment and technologies in order to improve their overall effectiveness while working.

Motivate Generation Z In The Workplace – Make Them An Individual Contributor

It is well known that members of Generation Z have an entrepreneurial spirit and a penchant for working independently. The majority of Gen Z workers would rather contribute to the organization on an individual basis, despite the fact that they have no trouble working in teams. They will have the opportunity to demonstrate their abilities if they are given the chance to work independently. In addition, they are driven by appreciation, and they take pride in being recognized for the work that they have accomplished. Therefore, keeping the motivation of members of Generation Z is not difficult; the important thing is to acknowledge and recognize the contributions they make.

How Generation Z's Personality Manifests In The Workplace

These young adults entering employment are extremely competitive and like the opportunity to test themselves against others. As a result of their upbringing in a competitive environment, they have acquired this characteristic. Therefore, they seek input. Encourage healthy rivalry among employees, particularly during the training phase, to keep Gen Zers engaged; you can keep young employees motivated and help them do their best work.

Gen Z In Comparison To Other Generations

Understanding the differences in work ethic, approach to authority, and preference for collaboration between generations can go a long way toward making everyone more effective at their jobs.

The Silent Generation

One word that comes to mind to define the work ethic of the Silent Generation is "committed." Even if someone is feeling ill or simply does not want to go to work, quitting their job or missing work is not an option for people of this age. They have a healthy reverence for those in positions of authority and respect hierarchical structures. The boss is usually held in extremely high regard. If, while at work, you noticed your supervisor approaching you for a discussion, it was probably a bad day, and you would probably not retain your job.

The Baby Boomers

The baby boomer generation has a reputation for having a strong work ethic because they came of age during a period in which the economy was flourishing and opportunities were abundant. In contrast to their predecessors from earlier periods in history, a sizable number of members of this generation were able to pursue higher education in addition to their careers. Never before have so many women and people of color held positions of leadership and degrees of higher education.

Because of this, they have respect not just for the act of working but also for official qualifications and credentials. Their attitude toward those in positions of authority is one of extremes, encompassing both love and hatred.

A manager in the healthcare industry who has an open shift is aware that if they call in, a boomer is quite likely to report for work. Because of this, many supervisors had a tendency to rely on them far more than they did on members of prior generations.

Generation X

It is less likely that a member of Generation X will come in to fill the identical empty shift that was described earlier. Despite the fact that Gen Xers still have a strong work ethic, they are more aware of the importance of maintaining a healthy work-life balance. Many members of this group represented the first generation of their families in which both of their parents held jobs outside the home. Their fathers were working 55 to 75 hours a week, which negatively affected their ability to spend time with their families. Some of these issues eventually led to divorce.

The members of Generation X have taken stock of their lives and decided, "I'm not going to be that person." That is why they want a work-life balance. These employees are more impressed by the leaders who put in the extra effort and are competent in their roles than they are by credentials.

Millennials

When it comes to their employment, Millennials have a strong sense of determination. There is no way to stop a millennial worker from achieving their goals if they are clear about what they want to do.

They have been encouraged to speak their minds and to have their voices heard. There is no such thing as being impolite when it comes to the desire to have input on virtually anything related to their professions. They are merely expressing their opinions and having a discussion about the topics they consider significant. It's possible that their leaders are the only ones who aren't used to discussing decisions through a conversation.

Millennials are renowned for their innate capacity to collaborate. They like lending a hand to one another without giving any consideration to what they could get in return. They are more capable of multitasking than anyone else, and they are quite clever when it comes to technology. They are hardwired to cooperate with each other. These workers are often tenacious and have a very positive outlook on what they are capable of doing.

Generation Z

Generation Z is comparable to the Millennials who came before them, except they have a shorter attention span and fewer interpersonal skills than their predecessors do. On the other hand, they are exceptionally skilled at technology and creativity.

They have an extremely open mind and are highly receptive to feedback given to them. They are eager for accolades and acknowledgment, but they do not place as much value on monetary compensation.

This demographic is interested in having a lifestyle that is adaptable and gives them the freedom to do anything they like. They are seeking a position that values their creativity and values face-to-face contact as well as working in teams.

CHAPTER SEVEN
Gen Z's View On Money

While every generation is unique in its own way, the Z generation is Shaping up to be the one that will recreate the world of finance.

This generation needs to be able to adapt in order to meet the challenges that have been brought about by both the present and past generations. The fact that they are acclimating and adjusting at a much faster speed than was anticipated is the peculiar part about it.

Generation Z experiences fears and issues that are left over from earlier generations. Many of them saw how their parents, who were members of Generation X, had difficulty making ends meet because of the Great Recession.

Even though many of them had stable jobs and enough money to get by, they couldn't weather the storm that the economic slump caused.

Gen Z also observed Millennials as they struggled to adapt to the advent of new technology. They observed the financial impact brought on by those who placed a higher priority on spending without being aware of the repercussions of their choices.

They were able to see the benefits of their efforts to pay off their school loans. The need for financial planning was something that a good number of Millennials learned the hard way on their own.

> 66 ——————————————————————————————
> *Members of Generation Z consider financial difficulties to be their biggest obstacle.*
> ——————————————————————————————— 99

The members of Generation Z have never experienced a time before the widespread use of mobile devices and the internet. It made it possible for them to quickly change and adapt. They witnessed how difficult it was for Millennials to pursue their aspirations due to the limited number of work opportunities. Many people, whether they are students or working professionals, put supply and demand at the top of their priority list.

They are also not so keen on taking on debt, with the majority choosing higher education options that are less expensive. While Millennials are better at putting money away, Gen Z is more responsible with their finances. As many people can attest to this in the present day, the younger generation enters the scene with experience to draw on, making them a more mature and formidable adversary.

According to data gathered from a study, the difference is as follows:

-        35% of members of Generation Z are already running their own businesses or have business plans in place.

-        Only 21% of members of Generation Z are interested in taking out educational debt.

-        64% of members of Generation Z have begun conducting research and having conversations with others on the need for financial planning.

-        75% of all members of Generation Z are open to relocating to a different state in the event of a job opportunity.

Financial Literacy

The concept of financial literacy is more than just a buzzword for workers in the Gen Z generation. It is something they have their sights set on as they move forward into the future.

One of the ways in which people of this new generation behave differently is that they are increasingly concerned about their own personal finances. A sizable majority of Gen Zers are aware of the importance of financial literacy and are motivated to improve their skills in this area.

However, determining where they got their information is one of the most difficult tasks they face. An estimated eighty-four percent still get their information about money matters from their parents and other family members.

> *Although Gen Z has a healthy attitude towards debt, there is a possibility that they are putting a lid on their potential by not taking on any.*

Although it might be useful to some extent, the information might be entirely incorrect, out of date, or missing important parts. The previous generations were forced to discover things the hard way. Some people continue to have the same misunderstandings. Even if members of Generation Z are starting to learn at a younger age than previous generations, they still need to expand their horizons.

The use of the internet is one of the ways in which they can accomplish this goal. The web offers access to an abundance of resources that can be utilized. Because there is so much information available, sorting the useful pieces of data from the rest of it is the most important step.

The good news is that today's young people are intelligent enough to know when something they read or watch online is authentic. Gen Zs are not the kinds of people who are likely to fall for cons and are adept at navigating the internet to achieve their goals.

Although Gen Z has a healthy attitude towards debt, there is a possibility that they are putting a lid on their potential by not taking on any.

They need education on how to properly handle debt and how to make responsible use of things like credit cards. Although there is a portion of the population that is already comfortable, the vast majority of people are still gaining knowledge.

> 66
>
> *Millennials and Gen Z invest in stocks and crypto currencies at rates that are comparable to one another, with approximately one quarter of Gen Z investing in crypto currencies.*
>
> 99

GEN Z Takes Financial Responsibility Seriously

The oldest members of Gen Z appear to have a strong grasp on the concept of financial responsibility. In a recent survey, 75% of respondents regularly save money, and over ten percent of them make payment in parts for their own homes.

These members of Generation Z are only now beginning their careers and maturing into adults. The fact that they have already begun saving is encouraging for both their long-term financial well-being and their readiness to become financially responsible.

In addition, 19.9% are those who are saving for an emergency fund, those who are saving simply to save are about 13.8%, and those who are saving to pay off debt are 10.6%. They are all taking measures to place themselves in a better financial position early in life. If they do this, it could put them in a better position to buy a house, get married or achieve a huge milestone.

Generation Z Hopes To Become Homeowners In Five Years

It has been said that Millennials were the generation that would always rent their homes, but it appears that members of Generation Z, often known as Zoomers, do not intend to continue in this tradition.

According to a recent study conducted by some realtors, among individuals in the Generation Z age bracket of 18 to 24, 86% have their sights set on homeownership, and of those individuals, 45% intend to own a home within the next five years. If these first-time homebuyers were successful in accomplishing this goal, they would be between the ages of 23 and 29 when they made their first house purchase.

Despite the fact that this may give the impression that Gen Z has an unduly positive view, the data shows that they are aware that they have their job cut out for them and see a number of potential problems on the horizon, but they also see very substantial rewards.

Members Of Generation Z Consider Financial Difficulties To Be Their Biggest Obstacle

Although the ambitious time frame for Gen Z home purchases may make their future appear promising, they are aware that the path will not be an easy one.

When asked what would make it the hardest for them to buy a house, 73.9 percent of respondents said financial constraints, with the following reasons given:

-       It is estimated that 21.9% of this group do not believe they will have sufficient funds for a down payment.

-       18.4% are skeptical that they will be able to locate a home priced within their budgetary constraints.

-       16.1% of the members of Generation Z are concerned about their lack of sufficient credit.

-       10.5% are concerned about having too much debt from college loans.

-      7% of people find the process of qualifying for a mortgage to be intimidating.

It's possible that the individuals who reported having trouble locating a house in their price range are aware of the supply limits that have prevented first-time homebuyers from entering the market.

It was found that about 81% of respondents in the Gen Z age bracket have an incorrect perception of how much it costs to own a home.

The good news is that members of Gen Z have options available to them to help them mitigate some of the challenges that lie ahead. Programs and grants are available, similar to those that were offered to previous generations of Millennials, to make homeownership more affordable.

Because Generation Z has such a strong desire to become homeowners, we can anticipate that there will be a large demand for these resources once they are brought to their attention.

Taxes

According to a survey, the younger members of Generation Z have a greater interest in learning about taxes when their income is lower. The widespread conviction that the funds allocated to Social Security will eventually be depleted is one element that has been proposed as a possible explanation for Gen Z's preoccupation with taxes. 43% say they can imagine a time when Social Security will no longer exist. Nearly one fifth of people say it's not at all likely that Social Security will be available to them when they retire.

Another possible explanation is that, as a result of the rise of the gig economy, a greater number of self-employed or entrepreneurially minded Gen Zers are interested in starting their own firms, which can result in problematic tax issues.

Investments

Gen Z is big on investment. 54% of members of Generation Z currently have investments of some type, such as equities, crypto currencies, or non-fungible tokens (NFTs).

It is important to note that investment is done by members of Gen Z from a diverse variety of demographics. The percentage of Gen Z women who have invested is about 48%, whereas the percentage of Gen Z men who have assets is 60%.

One factor that does differentiate members of Generation Z is income. Only 45% of people whose annual income is less than $50,000 are investing any of their money. In comparison, 73% of those with incomes of more than fifty thousand dollars have invested some of their money in various financial instruments.

New financial innovations, such as crypto currency, are the most popular areas of investment for Generation Z, just as they were for Millennials.

What They Invest In

A poll conducted by Motley Fool in April 2021 looked into the specific types of assets that appeal to Generation Z.

-       73% of Millennials have some form of stock ownership, making it the most prevalent form of investment for this generation.

-       The most common types of equity held by investors are growth stocks, dividend stocks, and value stocks, with growth stocks coming in first and dividend stocks coming in second.

-       Crypto currency ranks highly as well, with 47% of members of Generation Z holding onto this new asset class.

-       Only 30% of respondents stated that they hold at least one meme stock, despite the fact that they frequent Reddit; this indicates that meme stocks are not as commonly used as they once were.

-       It turns out that, according to the survey conducted by the Motley Fool, just 25% of Gen Z and Millennials reported owning ESG stocks, and 32% reported not knowing what an ESG stock is. This is in contrast to the results of a poll conducted by McKinsey Research, which found that 90% of members of Gen Z believe that companies "have a responsibility to address environmental and social issues."

-       When it comes to industries, the financial services industry was the one that was held by the most people at 42%, followed by the technology sector at 40%, and high-tech and emerging tech industries at 38%.

-       Only 35% of members of Generation Z invest in mutual funds, compared to 47% of Millennials. Meanwhile, only 15% of Generation Z members use exchange-traded funds, compared to 23% of Millennials.

- 30% of members of Generation Z have assets in bonds.

- 39 % of respondents say they possess stock options.

- Index funds are utilized by 22% of investors.

> 6 6 ————————————————
> *While every generation is unique in its own way, the Z generation is reshaping the world of finance.*
> ————————————————— 9 9

One-Fourth Of Gen Z, Millennials, And Gen X Use Crypto

As younger generations develop a skepticism about traditional investing, crypto and NFTs have emerged as popular investment tools to meet the needs of this age.

Some of their worries center on the fact that the government constantly seems to easily print more money whenever the economy begins to show signs of slowing down.

Millennials and Gen Z invest in stocks and crypto currencies at rates that are comparable to one another, with approximately one quarter of Gen Z investing in crypto currencies.

The percentage of males who possess crypto currencies and NFTs is roughly twice as high as that of women. However, these financial products can be especially susceptible to changes in the market. Spreading out the acquisition of your assets across a variety of other investments that are more secure and dependable is one strategy you may use to reduce the likelihood of taking on an excessive amount of risk.

PART THREE

CHAPTER EIGHT
Conversing With Them

A young mother came to see me in tears, worried at the demanding and hostile behavior of one of her Generation Z kids, named Ethan, who was only 19 years old at the time. Her second daughter, who was 17 years old, had gotten a scholarship, and she was expected to write certain exams to qualify for her new class.

Although she did not need so much inspection and help in studying, she still required more attention at the time. The mother started making it a duty to ensure she studied for the number of hours required by her teacher.

She said she made sure her daughter's food and required items for the day were taken directly to her room. She also monitored her general time with her friends who came to visit. She started spending her weekends with her daughter. Her husband also joined to help their daughter on weekends.

In the space of the three months that all this was happening, the actions and reactions of their son were totally unacceptable. He was usually quiet at home, and he spent most of his time online.

He was not interacting with anyone at home. Her Gen Z son had become steadily more demanding, and in the few weeks that followed, he had started lashing out at both his mother and his sister, even when neither of them had done anything to provoke him.

The mother said that during some of her son's angry outbursts, he would sometimes look at her very intently, as if he were almost waiting to see how the situation made her feel. She appeared baffled and confused as she described her son's behavior.

After listening to her talk, I asked, "So, what exactly do you think Ethan was feeling that led to his angry outbursts?" She appeared surprised at the question. She pursed her lips and did not speak for a moment.

Then she replied, "Well, I really don't know what he was feeling. I just know he was trying to make an impression!"

As the conversation continued, I helped her see how much Ethan must have felt neglected. Then she slowly began to realize how challenging it must have been for him to compete with his sister for parental attention.

A vast majority of parents have a sincere desire to be the best parents they can be, but they are left feeling baffled, confused, and hurt when, despite their efforts, things appear to go wrong.

Sometimes it looks like the approach of relating to the previous generation seems to have no effect when applied to Gen Z.

I am aware that parents have the capacity to comprehend and successfully navigate even the most challenging of scenarios and forms of communication. However, given the hectic nature of their day-to-day lives, they occasionally require the assistance of another person in order to carry out their parental duties or communicate better with their children.

Very often, a relative or a close friend will fill this position; but, when "an ordinary problem" becomes "exceptional," it may be necessary to get help from a trained professional.

When parents come to me, at times they may be worried and guilty that they have failed their children, as well as concerned that there is something wrong with either themselves or their child. My experience has taught me that none of this may be the case most of the time. Instead, most families who come to me for help have just gotten themselves confused. My role is to clear things up for them and make sense of this mess.

The narrative of Generation Z is representative of both my work and the purpose of this book, and particularly this chapter, which is to depict scenarios in such a way as to provide parents with the tools necessary to deal with their children in this age bracket. A lot of parents have gone for consultations with the wrong mindset.

To think of children's behavior solely in terms of "good or bad," "acceptable or unsuitable," and, consequently, merely as something that has to be controlled, is to think of it in a restricted manner, because this way, both the parent and the child will be at crossways. I hope that this aspect of the book will give you a fuller and more realistic picture of how to think about a child's behavior. This chapter will help you understand how to interact with and relate to Gen Zs around you.

Adults, according to a certain researcher, have a "sound parenting instinct."

That is a confusing suggestion! What we call instincts are frequently a blend of our natural tendencies, experimentation, and lessons learned from our parents. Bringing up a child is a difficult task. It is a bit of an experiment. This chapter does not provide a step-by-step guide on how to properly raise a Gen Z kid; rather, it provides ideas for activities and approaches that parents could use.

> 66 ——————————————————
> *You need to have real-time conversations with your Gen Z. Several issues can be resolved by simply communicating with them.*
> ——————————————— 99

It is hypothesized that the majority of parents can connect with a "sound instinct" that tells them what to do, i.e., an immediate way to respond to their children's behavior, if they are given time and space to ponder on the topic. The issue comes when a parent's "good instinct" and the demands of a certain child do not coincide completely.

Then, a parent may feel helpless, as if they are fumbling, as if they lack "good instinct" for parenting, and they may have a strong sense that "the books do not work!" You will remember your own childhood through being a parent, but you won't be able to change it.

REV. 3/11

ADVICE TO INTERNATIONAL PASSENGERS ON CARRIER LIABILITY

Passengers on a journey involving an ultimate destination or a stop in a country other than the country of departure are advised that international treaties known as the Montreal Convention, or its predecessor, the Warsaw Convention, including its amendments, may apply to the entire journey, including any portion thereof within a country. For such passengers, the treaty, including special contracts of carriage embodied in applicable tariffs, governs and may limit the liability of the carrier in respect of death of or injury to passengers, and for the destruction or loss of, or damage to, baggage, and for the delay of passengers and baggage. For additional information on international baggage liability limitations, including domestic portions of international journeys, see AA.com.

NOTICE OF INCORPORATED TERMS OF CONTRACT

Air Transportation, whether it is domestic or international (including domestic portions of international journeys), is subject to the individual terms of the transporting air carriers, which are herein incorporated by reference and made part of the contract of carriage. Other carriers on which you may be ticketed may have different conditions of carriage. International air transportation, including the carrier's liability, may also be governed by applicable tariffs on file with the U.S. and other governments and by the Warsaw Convention, as amended, or by the Montreal Convention. Incorporated terms may include, but are not restricted to: 1. Rules and limits on liability for personal injury or death, 2. Rules and limits on liability for baggage, including fragile or perishable goods, and availability of excess valuation charges, 3. Claim restrictions, including time periods in which passengers must file a claim or bring an action against the air carrier, 4. Rights on the air carrier to change terms of the contract, 5. Rules on reconfirmation of reservations, check-in times and refusal to carry, 6. Rights of the air carrier and limits on liability for delay or failure to perform service, including schedule changes, substitution of alternate air carriers or aircraft and rerouting.

You can obtain additional information on items 1 through 6 above at any U.S. location where the transporting air carrier's tickets are sold. You have the right to inspect the full text of each transporting air carrier's terms at its airport and city ticket offices. You also have the right, upon request, to receive (free of charge) the full text of the applicable terms incorporated by reference from each of the transporting air carriers. Information on ordering the full text of each air carrier's terms is available at any U.S. location where the air carrier's tickets are sold. Additionally, American Airlines' contract terms are found on AA.com under the "Legal" link. You can reach American Airlines on the web, using the following link: www.aa.com/customerrelations.

PRINTED IN U.S.A. BY MAGNETIC TICKET AND LABEL CORP., DALLAS, TX   REV. 2/11   CPN1113922

PASSENGER TICKET AND BAGGAGE CHECK
SUBJECT TO CONDITIONS OF CONTRACT

ISSUED BY

AMERICAN AIRLINES
oneworld

NAME OF PASSENGER (NOT TRANSFERABLE)

X/O FROM
NYAGWOKA / JOYCE
TO
KANSAS CITY / JOYCE
X/O
PHILADELPHIA

ENDORSEMENTS/RESTRICTIONS

ORIGINAL ISSUE

FARE CALCULATION

FARE

TAX/FEE/CHARGE

TAX/FEE/CHARGE

TAX/FEE/CHARGE

TOTAL

MAIN

STOCK CONTROL NUMBER TX
0013042603 5640

CARR.   FLIGHT   CLASS   DATE   TIME
NCE /MCI
AA 1619   G   13NOV   150P
KANSAS CITY INT

MIS/AGENT ID
13NOV22

US

BOARDING PASS
BOARDING ENDS 15 MINUTES
BEFORE DEPARTURE

ISSUED IN EXCHANGE FOR

GROUP 5
SEAT 8F

PNR CODE

PNR CODE
TTVUSV TKY MA

COUPON   AIRLINE

SEQ. NO.   ALLOW   PCS   CK. WT.   UNCK. WT.

3 001-2348175113 3

ISO
FOR
NCE /MCI

NAME OF PASSENGER

AMERICAN AIRLINES
BOARDING PASS

X/O FROM
NYAGWOKA / JOYCE
TO
KANSAS CITY INTL
X/O
PHILADELPHIA

REVALIDATION
CARRIER   FLIGHT   CLASS   DATE   TIME
AA 1619   G   13NOV   150P

GATE
84

ADDITIONAL SEAT INFORMATION
120P
BOARDING TIME

SEAT
8F
NO
SMOKE

COUPON   AIRLINE
BAGGAGE ID NR.   PCS   CK. WT.   UNCK. WT.

SEQ. NO.   PCS   CK. WT.   UNCK. WT.
FORM SERIAL NO.

GROUP 5

CK

Also, you cannot consider the difficulties and tribulations of your own childhood as a major determinant of your child's.

During the initial session with Ethan's mother, she had made a list of his problematic habits. I did some investigating and found out that most of the contention stemmed from Ethan's refusal to have any form of conversation with his family members. He continued acting out towards his parents because he believed they neglected him. In an effort to create time for him and have family bonding time, his parents decided to have a family picnic every other month. Despite the efforts of his parents, Ethan was not having it.

His parents continued to be considerate and reasonable, trying to reach out to him, yet every time he was told to go talk to his sister and choose a picnic time, he totally refused. When the time that had been set aside for the picnic arrives, Ethan will create a new ruckus for no apparent reason.

There were times his sister had gone to meet him to try to iron things out, but he would stay mute no matter how long she talked. He preferred to stay up all night chatting with friends on his phone. It was at this point that his parents decided to discipline him.

As a form of punishment, Ethan was compelled to go to sleep as soon as 9:30 p.m. However, during the first three nights, Ethan stayed up way past 9:30pm, and because of this, he was also required to stay with his sister for an hour each day. All this did not change anything. Instead, Ethan grew colder towards his sister by the day.

Ethan's parents thought they were able to eliminate a source of contention in one facet of their son's anger management. They thought they were able to think creatively about how to cope with other challenges that came up throughout Ethan's adolescence, but they were wrong!

It turned out that they weren't adequately prepared for what was happening.

During the phase of their family rift, they had relocated. Ethan met kids his age in the new neighborhood. He made friends with them and started visiting them in their homes. Everything changed when he saw how his new friends and their parents interacted. He also noticed that his friends had some degree of freedom. This influenced how he started reacting at home. He started comparing his own parents to those of his friends.

He saw his parents as disrespectful to him, and he didn't see a need to comply with the instructions given to him. And as time went by, his relationship with his family deteriorated.

Ethan's mother also narrated how her husband did not usually have time to communicate with Ethan. All he had time to do was to lay down rules for Ethan to obey. Ethan's parents believed the rules were a form of communication. Ethan also got accustomed to those rules and just automatically anticipated punishment whenever he did not adhere to them.

How can parents get it right?

What really is a parent's sound instinct, and where does it come from?

Where and how might an individual get the necessary training to become a parent?

When do the so-called "parental instincts" kick in?

People often think that both men and women know how to be parents from the time they are born.

As demonstrated by Ethan's parents, our society is riddled with notions about what is "good for children." These myths about child raising, like all myths, have their origins in fact, but they are often misunderstood and misapplied.

It's possible that the guidance offered (whether it's asked for or not!) by grandparents to parents, friends to friends, and experts to parents can perpetuate the idea that there's only one proper way to raise children.

It is especially important to remember that punishment and rules cannot replace communicating with adult children, especially with Generation Z. There has to be proper and healthy communication.

I will address three basic ways of parenting Gen Z. I practically use these ways to parent my kids and those I am mentoring. The parents I counsel also use these ways, and we have gotten fantastic results with our Gen Z kids.

Ethan's mother did not know that what she needed to do was basically communicate with him.

Most of the time, complaints cause rifts in relationships.

Rather than complaining to him about how distant he was, it was more important to have had a conversation with him and to apologize for not giving him quality time. She could have spelled out the reasons why it seemed like the whole family's energy and attention was totally directed towards his sister. Such that, He would see reasons with her and also come to understand that the same attention would be given to him too if he was in that situation.

I believe if someone feels neglected, the right response should be to show him or her that he is wrong about feeling that way or apologize if he was truly neglected. They wouldn't have had to come see a professional if they were able to talk it out and hug it out like my little kid likes to emphasize.

> *The vast majority of parents have a genuine desire to be the best parents they can be, and they are left feeling baffled when, in spite of their efforts, things appear to go wrong, because it seems like Generation Z is such a different generation.*

Engage In Face-To-Face Dialogue

You need to have real-time conversations with your Gen Z. Several issues have been resolved by simply communicating with them. Although some Gen Z kids did not totally agree, they chose to align. Just by conversing, I allow my Gen Z to bare their minds, and then I proceed to offer my views. I sometimes explain the rules, not intending to bend them but to cause them to view things differently. This works tremendously.

It Is A Major Issue That We Have No Idea How To Communicate With Our Gen Z Children.

It is simple to attribute Generation Z's affinity for internet communication to the fact that they grew up with it. You know that kids who grew up with Nintendo DSs, Club Penguin, iPod Touches, and Minecraft are very good with technology. However, it is more than just comfort. To understand Generation Z, or young adults, you have to understand that economic, political, terrorist, and pandemic anxiety are in their genes.

Unlike in the past, the recent dark decades were not just endured; they were deeply absorbed, changing how millions of people now feel, think, and talk to each other. Even though 85 percent of young adults prefer RL (real-life, or away-from-keyboard) engagement to build relationships, three-fifths of them think it's easier to express themselves online than in person. They want to live without a keyboard, but they also want the "superpowers" or wide range of expression that technology gives them.

To Understand Gen Z Is To Understand Language

Bernard's mom sent a screenshot of her chat with Bernard to me. She had explained how, after asking him questions, he would reply with a word and a smiley. She was totally confused by the smileys. Looking at the smiley, one could tell he was on the edge. I mean, there were hints and parts of the chat that should have gotten her worried if she understood the smiley sent. So, when I explained what all the smileys meant, she was just quiet and angry. I could tell she was angry with herself for failing to see the signs before things got out of hand.

Smileys are like an integral part of Gen Z's way of communicating. You could almost tell the mood of a Gen Z kid from their chat and choice of smileys. Bernard's mum saw how many sad smileys her son had used in the space of a few lines of chat. He had expressed himself for so long about how he felt about his cousin staying in his room. He was not able to talk to his dad because it was his dad's idea to have him share a room with his cousin. In the chat, he was explaining his situation to his mum; how it was almost impossible for his cousin to keep a neat room.

This has really affected his relationship with his cousin because at first he would complain a lot and his cousin would be very upset. So, he didn't want to keep complaining. He decided to keep mute and watch. He is actually very used to a clean room, so seeing his room dirty made him sad.

One day, Bernard went to his friend's house. He sent a message to his parents later in the evening, that he would spend the night there. His dad had an argument with him over it as he did not approve. But Bernard stayed regardless. It was that night that Bernard's emotions were heightened and he let out all that he had bottled up about his sadness to his mother. In the heat of the moment, Bernard returned home the next morning, he packed his things and moved out of his parents' house and continued to stay with his friend. Since then, he stopped communicating with his parents regularly.

Away from home, Bernard had room to explore. He went out more often and joined a tech-savvy Gen Z forum. There he learned how to develop software for mobile applications. He successfully developed a gaming software for mobile after his

9 months of training, and that earned him such a huge contract worth more than his parents' savings account could hold for the next decade. After some time, he found a business that he could collaborate with to promote the gaming application.

He had so much money that he could now afford to buy his own house. He invited his parents over to see his new home. While he showed them around, they barely spoke to each other. The strain on their relationship was obvious. His father expressed disapproval. He told Bernard he was too young to have this kind of freedom and space. Bernard ignored everything his father said and concluded in his mind that he would never talk to his father again.

Ever since that experience, his mum has been trying to understand what happened and how they failed to keep a good relationship with Bernard. She realized that she really did not understand how to communicate with him.

And she couldn't be more correct.

There was a lack of good and productive communication with Bernard.

His parents, like every other parent, struggle to understand Generation Z's conversational patterns. After going through the stress of work each day and getting back home to try to fix food for the family, they are already too exhausted to strike up a conversation with their children. Some parents even have to bring work home from the office in order to meet deadlines. The result of this kind of busy life is that relationships will suffer badly.

That is why it is important to talk to our Gen Z kids clearly and regularly. You must understand their chat patterns so that you are not lost in your communication with them. A lot of parents usually ask their children if they understand them. But they don't usually try to understand their children.

Communication Is About Understanding

No matter what you say to the Gen Z kids and no matter how many times you say it, you can't force them to communicate with you. You can't force them to talk to you if you do not understand them.

I remember a father and son moment I had with one of my children. It was one of the moments when he told me almost everything I didn't even think I would know. I caught him in the sitting room one midnight talking on the phone. I listened to the conversation for a while before walking towards the kitchen to get a glass of water. Once he saw me walk past him, he ended his call abruptly and looked very tense.

"You remind me of my younger self," I said to him, with a broad smile on my face.

He relaxed.

"Carry on", I encouraged. "Don't forget to get some sleep early enough."

He nodded, and I said, "My regards to your friend."

That night started what I can refer to as our best bonding phase.

I guess he was expecting me to scold him for staying up till that time. I figured he was talking to a girl, and I didn't even ask him who he was speaking with.

I know he saw me differently that night. I was paving my way to becoming his buddy—not just a dad, but a friend he could tell absolutely anything. It is very important that you know what being a parent means to your kid.

Parenting Generation Z means that you have to become their friend, their advisor, and their teacher. It's all about giving and taking. You don't demand that they communicate with you, but rather you initiate communication. One way to initiate conversation with them is by sharing your experiences with them.

Most of the time, I share experiences with the children I mentor and listen to them. I've realized that when we share as friends rather than superiors, we accomplish more.

This generation has a unique perspective on communication. They differ greatly from previous generations. In fact, we have never encountered someone who shares their perspective.

Do You Genuinely Understand What Various Emojis Mean?

Young adults are more inclined to share memes than selfies or food photos on social media. Why? The meme provides more emotion than textual information. The meme contains cultural information that serves as a secondary message. What is conveyed is securely delegated to a character. Memes communicate profound collective truths.

And in a world when time is limited, visual representations are easier to access and consume. They will not disappear. Over time, knowing how memes work has become more and more important, and this trend seems to be getting stronger. Everything is content, and Generation Z communicates with varying forms of content.

When Generation Z posts a photo or video, it means something completely different from what it means to other generations. For a generation whose feelings are so subtle and complex, these non-verbal but lively ways to express them are essential. If you want to be a part of their future, whether as a direct or indirect recipient, you have to figure out what their mode of communication is.

What You Should Know About Generation Z

Generation Z is the biggest group in the US at the moment, and they have a big impact on how our economy works. Parents who take the time to understand Generation Z and improve their emotional and communication skills win.

Those who have these skills will thrive, appeal to this generation, and will have great peace. Companies spend time to understand what appeals to this set. Parents should also do this, because it's best to take time to understand how to get through to them.

We should also know that, with Generation Z playing an increasing role in driving our country's economy, the last thing to do as a form of punishment is slash their allowance.

The process of parents' using slash in allowance as a form of communication with these young adults is almost ineffective. You may not even know that your child is already developing software for companies, or engaging in freelance jobs, and getting paid.

How To Start Conversations With Generation Z

If you're trying to start a conversation with your Gen Zer and want to know how to earn their loyalty, you must understand how to successfully start conversations with them. You need to understand what makes the other person tick in order to have a productive conversation. I mentioned earlier how I saw my son speaking on the phone with his friend, who I guessed was a female friend.

My reaction to that incident got him to open up to me and even come straight to me for advice afterwards.

I had heard the sound of his door on another occasion, and I gave him a couple of minutes to go to the sitting room before I left my room.

I walked into the kitchen and filled up a glass of water to drink. I started looking for different things to do to pass the time. Eventually, he finished his call a little faster than expected. I guess he had seen me doing things in the kitchen.

As I walked past him to return to my room, he said, "Hello, dad."

I responded, "Hello, son."

"I see that you keep speaking to your friend at night," I said.

He smiled shyly.

I told him, "I have been there."

I started talking to him about my friendships when I was his age and what I thought I did right and wrong. It was my way of advising him without trying to be too intrusive.

He later told me his friend's name and how he had been her friend for a while. In fact, he said more than I expected him to. That day, I could feel our bond strengthening. We were beginning to get more intimate by the day. And the reason is not far-fetched: we started having real conversations.

Conversing with Generation Z is a two-way street. I got more from my kid because I also opened up, and our relationship is better for it.

It is imperative as parents to have real conversations with our Gen Z children. They are very smart and fast. They have real conversations when they hang out with their friends, and there they talk about anything and everything, including the things they learn about in the online space. It would be rewarding for both you and your children if you could engage in having real conversations with them.

You should learn to use conversation as a way to bond with your children.

Conversing with them is not just about scolding them and questioning their every move. While you can ask questions during conversations, you must know the right time for it.

For example, if I want to have a conversation with my child with the intent of knowing if he is having problems with bullies at school, I could start by telling him how my school days were and how there were bullies in my school that I was scared of and the things I did to overcome that fear. If I ask him afterwards if he is having problems with bullies in school, I'm positive that he will be more willing to share his experiences with me than if I asked him directly if he was having bullying problems.

Sometimes these Generation Z just prefer to talk to interact among themselves because there is no superior or someone putting them on the spot with questions they are not in the mood to answer. So, as a parent, you will sometimes have to be very patient and build up the conversation gradually by sharing your experiences with them and seeking to bond with them. That will encourage them to give you the answers that you need to hear from them.

Some years ago, Mr. and Mrs. Carson brought their son, Nathan, to me for a session.

They had complained that they had been seeing him sad constantly, and they considered it to be related to school. So, they kept asking Nathan what happens to him when he goes to school. Every time they asked him, he looked sadder and always gave them the same response: "There is nothing wrong happening in school."

It's always the same answer.

At some point, they even had to go to his school to ask questions, but they were not able to gather anything meaningful.

However, Mr. Carson still felt very strongly that the problem his son was having started at school.

I asked the parents to give me time with him. They left my office to go to the waiting room while he came in.

When he came in, he had a funny expression on his face. I smiled at him, but he didn't smile back.

His mum had seized his phone earlier in the car on their way to my office, because she felt he would be distracted by it if he came with it to my office. She had taken it out of her bag when it was ringing during our conversation and put it on the table after apologizing for the loud interruption.

"Sorry about that," she said. "It's a call on Nathan's phone, but I have muted it now."

Just before she stepped out of my office, I had told her to leave the phone behind. She looked at me, unsure if it was a good idea, but she went ahead and left it behind as requested.

"Your phone rang earlier." I said, handing him his phone. "You might want to return the call."

I excused myself into the adjourning room while he started dialing a number. I observed him through the glass wall while he talked on the phone.

As I stepped back into the office, I walked across to the shelf and switched on the television screen and the video game console.

"Let's move to the couch, Nathan," I said. He reluctantly stood up from the visitor's chair at my desk to join me.

I took a gamepad for myself and handed the other one to him, asking, "FIFA," or "Need for Speed?"

"FIFA," he replied, staring at me with intense curiosity as he slowly sat down on the couch.

Luckily for me, he didn't choose Need for Speed. I didn't know much about it. However, my son and I have played FIFA several times.

"How come you can play?" he asked.

"My son showed me the ropes, and since then, I play FIFA with him any chance I get," I responded, chuckling.

We exchanged small talk about football teams and their coaches. He gradually let down his guard, smiled a couple of times, and we even had some good-natured banter about the next football season starting later in the year.

We also talked about school football, and then I gradually steered the conversation into unhealthy competition in high school football and how some boys are even bullied by their teammates to quit playing when they realize they play better football than they do. I also talked about how I was bullied at some point too by a group of boys when I was in high school and how scared I was.

The next question he asked me suggested that he had a bullying problem.

"Did they also tell you they would hurt your family if you ever reported them?" He asked

"Yes", I answered.

"Did you report them after the threat?" He probed further.

"Yes, I still went ahead to report them," I responded.

"Then what happened to your loved ones?" Nathan asked.

I smiled as I said, "nothing".

"Nothing?!"

"Are you sure?" he asked.

"I should know if something happened, don't you think?" I responded.

"Did you transfer from the school to another school?" he quizzed.

"No." "I didn't need to," I replied.

It was at this point that Nathan opened up, and he started explaining how a bully gang had been hitting him after school, and how it was a constant thing they did. This is the reason he was always angry whenever he came back from school. At times, he would stay locked up in his room, crying. His parents feared that he was depressed.

Imagine their shock when they found out he was trying to protect them by not saying anything to them about his problems at school.

You see, at times, you might be doing the right thing the wrong way. This is the reason it looks like there is usually no result. Communication is the bedrock of your relationship with your child.

If you are going to be a part of their lives to teach, lead, and discipline them and get results, you have to be able to establish a good relationship with them.

This cannot be replaced by buying gifts or crediting their bank accounts. Neither is it the usual "how are you?" Question, with the usual "I am fine" answer.

Another client, Mrs. Anderson, came to my office the other day to talk to me about mentoring her daughter, Anna. She believed her daughter's priorities had changed and she needed the assistance of a professional to guide her in the right direction. A friend had recommended me to her.

After we exchanged pleasantries, I asked her to tell me about her typical daily schedule. Her schedule was all centered on work and having to cater to the financial obligations in the home and meeting the responsibilities of catering to the needs of her daughter alone as a single mother. I just listened to her speak:

I'm working extra hard because of her. She attends the best schools. A chauffeur drives her to and from school. Every time I get a new client, I increase her allowance. I started my own business solely to better provide for her. And, as you must already know, a CEO position entails a great deal of work and responsibilities. We also recently moved to a new neighborhood with better security.

When I started my business, her grades began to fall. I thought it was because of our new location, but it's only getting worse. Aside from her grades, she had changed drastically.

She called me two days ago to tell me she wanted me to meet someone. Can you imagine my surprise when she presented me with a boy?

He appeared to be nearing the end of his college career. My child is nearly sixteen years old. I recall her saying during one of our chit-chats that she will not consider getting into a relationship until she is at least 19 years old. When she said that, it made me happy. But she's here introducing me to a boy when she's only fifteen years old.

After the boy left, I told her I didn't approve, but she only replied by saying, "I don't care."

"I have been seeing him for nine months now," she added, as she walked away from me.

That put me in a state of shock. I could not imagine that she had kept this away from me for nine months.

I asked the chauffeur about her movements, and he explained that he usually drops her off at this boy's house, where she stays for a few hours before bringing her back home. I would occasionally drive both of them to our house, and the boy would stay until late at night, then leave minutes before you arrived.

This must have been the reason why she always called me at 7 o'clock in the evening to see whether I was coming home soon. I always just assumed she was checking in on me.

The chauffeur also thinks my daughter has been exposed to a number of inappropriate activities that I don't know about.

"Why didn't you tell me all these things?" I asked him, alarmed.

He replied, "You didn't ask me."

Mrs. Anderson ended her narration on this somber note: "I'm really sad and disappointed in myself because I've completely lost track of what's going on in my daughter's life."

I had the privilege of meeting Anna. My session with her revealed that before her mother got so caught up in her business, she relied heavily on her for emotional support. Her mother was her best friend. But she lost all that because her mother got so busy and stopped paying attention to her.

It turns out her boyfriend is the brother of one of her schoolmates. They'd gotten close since the first hello! He was always available, and she began to spend most of her time with him. For her, he filled the void that her mother's neglect left. But, unfortunately, she had picked up many bad habits from him that she now regrets. She also blamed her mother for being absent from her life. Anna was pregnant by the time she realized the guy wasn't right for her. Why did I share these experiences?

Sometimes the consequences of avoiding your children or being too busy to communicate with them are so severe that you wish you could go back in time and be there for them.

The Things You Should Know About Gen Z When Starting A Conversation With Them Are Itemized Below:

They Place The Highest Priority On Authenticity

Generation Z was raised with access to smartphones and every social media platform from a very young age. They have been taught how to create online communities with people they don't know and how to keep a presence online by using different social media platforms with various sorts of content. As a result, they believe they have a good idea of what a real relationship is.

Communicating with Generation Z necessitates a sense of humor that isn't overly filtered or false. They can tell when one is not being real with them. They have outlets like YouTube and TikTok as powerful tools to weigh authenticity. They will follow and value leaders who also value authenticity, so this is what we should look out for as parents.

Your children should look up to you as a role model, but if they cannot even see you as this, at least they should know you to be truthful and real.

They Promote Difficult Dialogue

Generation Z is made up of people who remember 9/11, grew up during the financial crisis of 2008, and grew up with school shootings as a terrible norm. They've lived through many wars, severely divided politics, the Black Lives Matter movement, a dangerously changing climate and a pandemic by the time they got to their teens or early twenties.

Topics such as mental health and social concerns in the country are not avoided, and many have a strong interest in politics and mental health. It won't be bad to do a bit of analysis with your child. You can pick up a topic about politics with your child and sample his or her opinions.

You should learn to do this as often as you can because the Gen Z kids like to be taken seriously. And don't forget that they have a lot of access to learning resources. You may be surprised when your child begins to open your eyes to new perspectives.

To talk to Gen Zers, you have to be willing to tell them the truth about hard problems and stand up for yourself when you have to. Even though it can be hard for college students to talk about politics, sharing educational materials on all social media platforms is a strong way to show unity with Gen Z's goals.

Also, they aren't afraid to use social media to start tough debates and talk about how upset they are. This means that having a sound crisis communication plan that focuses on how to establish bridges quickly is critical, as the fast-paced Gen Z doesn't want to wait for an answer to something they believe is clear and essential.

Children of Generation Z are likely to challenge their parents' beliefs and values. You can bet they'll want to know why you're making a specific request or imposing a specific punishment. Parents generally dislike being questioned, basically because when we were younger, it seemed inappropriate to question our parents because they had the last say.

This reminds me of Mrs. Davis, a friend of mine who struggled with raising her twenty-year old daughter, Adriana. According to her, her kid is nasty and hard to talk to. So I told her to tell Adriana to pay me a visit.

The week after, Adriana stopped by my workplace on her way to the grocery store. We had a lengthy discussion where we both expressed our thoughts and feelings on a variety of topics. Most of my convictions were called into question by Adriana, and I was pressed to offer detailed justification.

She asked, "Why?" quite frequently.

"Why did you refuse to let your kid buy a power bike?"

"Why do parents scold their kids when they get home late?"

"Please explain why you don't think young adults should be allowed to go to parties that last all night."

She asked a lot of questions, and I answered each one thoroughly. When we finished talking, she said she had a better perspective on some of her parents' decisions and opinions.

Before leaving, she turned around and asked, "Is it okay to come by another time to chat with you?"

I replied, "You are welcome anytime, Adriana."

"Conversation with you is different," she said. "I wish my parents would communicate with me like you did."

A while later, Mrs. Davis dropped by and inquired as to my opinion about her daughter. It was my duty to make her realize how remarkable her daughter is and how critical it is to understand that questions are an integral part of conversing with her child.

Kids are more likely to ask clarifying questions when they don't agree with or understand what you've said. We need to learn to be flexible and answer our kids' many questions so they don't look elsewhere for information.

Children who are curious and ask questions shouldn't be cast in a negative light. We should anticipate that our kids will ask "why?" whenever they have questions, and we should be ready to answer them.

CHAPTER NINE
Leading Them

Many parents will tell you that they are leading their children perfectly when they have not been leading them by example. Because Generation Z is a generation that runs on logic and experience, leading by example is the best way to raise your children. They are actually not interested in mere talk. Any action expected of them should be exemplified first. A lot of people still say that "what you say is what you get". That can't work when it comes to Gen Z. It's "what you do is what you get" with them.

I recently listened to a school administrator speak to parents before I walked on stage to do a presentation to those same parents on the most common mistakes we make as we lead our Gen Z today. The administrator attempted to encourage parents by saying

"No student will be permitted to go to the restroom without an adult."

All students must be accompanied by a "buddy" on the playground at all times.

"No students are allowed to walk or ride their bikes home after school."

Most of the parents nodded in agreement as the "safety first" rules were clarified. I suddenly realized I had my work cut out for me and knew I had to share some research if the evening was to end productively. I thought the point was to emphasize how we can be better leaders for these kids.

This is exactly what I meant when I said that enforcing laws and demanding respect is not the way to lead Generation Z. You cannot lead by laying down dos and don'ts. And I guess for most of the generations before now, it worked well. Our parents thought they were doing great work by reading to us or stating to us a thousand things we could do or not do. I mean, we did most of the things we were told not to do and had our ways of covering up our tracks. They couldn't even tell because their emotional intelligence quotient was below average.

If we try to bombard Generation Z with laws, their own response will be different. They don't follow you because you tell them to; they have to see a reason to. They choose the people they will follow. That means you have to prove to them that you are a leader for them to start following you. By that, I mean you have to prove it by being an example.

And another thing that is common is how parents believe they have to overly protect their Gen Z kid, to the point that the kid does not have any form of privacy. What parents tend to believe today is that being paranoid is actively looking out for their kids. It's a well-intentioned approach that's damaging to children.

It's based on the belief that our world has become very unsafe for young adults and that they should spend every waking hour under adult supervision. A lot of professionals expounded on how Gen Z's safety is a priority. A lot of people have begun devoting their time and life to creating means and ways to further protect their young adults from evil occurrences.

All of these were positive initiatives, but the negative, unintended consequences have been enormous. In this decade, adults began to believe our world was less safe than ever—and kids needed oversight or direction at all times. Many parents start over-parenting their children (young adults).

> **"**
> *Raising Gen Z today includes keeping in the back of your mind that children today are exposed to a lot of information.*
> **"**

What Was The Intended Result?

As children became a greater priority in our culture, societal shifts began happening.

Let me explain the outcomes from decades of research on this parenting style:

Gen Zs began feeling entitled to special perks because we said, "They're special."

Most of them begin to feel unsafe, afraid, and even paranoid because of their parents' behavior.

They began to believe they were frail and could not handle adversity, thereby embracing the narrative that the world is full of evil people who could harm them.

The fact is, the numbers show our world is actually safer for children today than it was when I was a kid. For example, in 2013, the data shows that the most violent crimes (murders) were lower than they ever were in the past.

Who would've known?

The difference is, we believe violent crimes are happening in and around our communities because of the 24/7 news cycle that reports such crimes and the social media feeds that arrive on our phones to overwhelm us and make us uber-cautious.

Quite frankly, parents' viewpoints are wildly out of sync with the realities of culture. Too many of us, to put it bluntly, are "paranoid parents."

Four Strategies For Parenting Generation Z

So let me suggest some parenting ideas you might use as you lead your young adults:

Don't Freak Out

We need to let our kids take appropriate risks in our "safety first" world, but when they choose something odd or even crazy, we need to stay calm. Whatever you do—don't freak out at the seemingly strange decisions teens feel empowered to make today. From tattoos to piercings to decisions about friends, kids growing up today are living in a very new world. If we don't react emotionally but talk to them respectfully, we earn the right to help them think through the long-term implications of their choices.

This is our role: wise and steady leadership. Equip them to think long-term; think big.

Acknowledge Them Accurately And Specifically

Generation Z kids are privy to the hyperbolic praise Millennials got from parents. Everything was described as "awesome"—even when it really wasn't. Adult leaders must be careful how they praise teens and should use words that accurately reflect what they did. They'll actually believe us if we do.

It is spot on.

And it's important to tell kids when they mess up. You can't keep saying awesome things that are not. There is no way the child will know that improvement is needed. You can say, "You did try, but it can be better, in fact a lot better."

Learn to also help them out when they are dealing with their failures. One major thing to know is that the reaction to failure will tell you if you will be able to move on from it positively or stay retarded because of it. You can reason it out together, analyzing what led to the failure and planning to avert it the next time.

Comments like "You tried your best," "Don't feel terrible, you can't do it," and "Don't worry, it's not your strength" can hold a child back, and this is especially true in this day and age. Generation Z is easily sidetracked or gives up when things get difficult.

On the other hand, comments such as "What can we attempt next time?" and "Don't feel bad if you can't do it yet," put the emphasis on a growth perspective. This is because they are thinking about how they can try something new next. Even though they didn't get what they wanted this time. It helps them with setting more challenging goals and provides parents with tangible ways to encourage their children to put in a lot of effort.

Be Clear About Their Equations

I discourage having a ton of "rules" and encourage you to remind kids of life's "equations." Equations are simply outcomes of wise or poor behavior: if you do this, that is the benefit; if you do that, this is the consequence.

As a result, students begin to learn that life is full of equations. Upon entering adulthood, you learn that if you don't pay your rent, you lose the apartment; if you do pay rent on time, you get to keep it. Such equations will educate generation Z kids about how the world works. Make the equations clear and be sure to follow up on them.

When my Gen Z son mentioned relationships, I remembered that I gave him the following advice: "I am not angry about you having a relationship, nor do I think the timing is bad. It will become bad when it becomes a source of distraction. If you now begin to give more time to your relationship, forgetting your studies, the consequences will be grave". I laid bare to him the consequence of such a distraction.

"Also, if you and your friend start having issues leading to emotional instability, which now affects your education and grade, the person to go through those consequences will be you," I added.

"If you and your friend decide to focus on your education and make sure you are not distracted, your good grades will be staring you in the face. And I am sure we will all be happy about that." It looked like I gave them a reason to study together. They both had amazing grades for that session.

Model Consistency

One of the most conspicuously absent elements in our world today is consistency. Nothing seems to be consistent—except inconsistency. Uncertainty is everywhere. Change happens all the time: couples divorce, jobs change, rules are updated, TV shows are canceled, and even our Internet connection can be spotty. Parents and teachers must be consistent in their verbal and visual cues. Kids feel secure when consistent leadership is exemplified.

If you are like the majority of parents, you realize that a lot has changed in our homes, especially when it comes to parenting and raising our children in the midst of the pandemic.

So much happened all at once: the pandemic, online learning, the Black Lives Matter movement and awareness, an increase in digital media use, video games, consumption, and so much more! The year 2020 had a lot of events. The consequences of the events of that year are still felt by some families to this date.

According to Wikipedia, children born between the mid-to-late 1990s and the early 2010s are "Generation Z". Even though members of Generation Z are called "digital natives," that doesn't mean they know how to use technology. This leaves them vulnerable to most online dangers.

Generation Z tends to be well-behaved and afraid of taking risks, but they are more likely to have mental health problems than previous generations.

How can we then ensure that our children have what it takes to survive and thrive in the 21st century?

Everyone is now online, and we need to talk about how to raise responsible digital citizens, with a focus on online safety and digital well-being. Some parents do not look at it as a serious thing to do. Your child has a computer in his room and at school. He also has access to the Internet on his phone all the time. And he asks you certain questions, and you reply with, "you cannot be asking about that now, it's beyond the scope of topics for your age bracket." But he has a phone, which gives him access to unlimited resources.

A young adult's access to the Internet must be checked and monitored because if we are really concerned about the safety of our kids, we need to start with online safety. You can't be so focused on the danger you believe they may face without checking their internet access. As parents, we need to make sure to teach our children the right values so that before they go online, they already know who they are and what they stand for.

This is because, for Gen Z, everything they find online is a direct attack on their identity. It's the new normal for them to be exposed to all this sort of information and content online.

As a result, they feel that they are being constantly judged and can easily feel out of place when the majority of people are doing something that they are not.

So, the most important lesson you need to teach is that, because everyone is doing something, it does not make it right. Likewise, because you are the only one doing a certain thing doesn't make it wrong.

Gen Z has a lot of access to information and sees what is happening at their fingertips. However, as parents, we can do so much more to contextualize what they're seeing. This places more responsibility on parents because you may not know, so you may also have to go out and do your research.

Raising Gen Z today includes keeping in the back of your mind that children today are exposed to a lot of information.

We know that this is the generation that is supposed to question everything. In the past, our generation, the older generation, came to believe many things over time without ever questioning or looking into them. Because our parents taught us these ideas when we were young, we didn't know if they were true or not. Also, when we found out that some of those things were wrong, we didn't dare question them because most people did them. We didn't dare go up to them because of this.

But we should know that the way generations before and after Gen Z use technology is very different from one another. This is because Gen Z grew up with technology. It is literally a part of their DNA. It's important to understand this when it comes to raising children from Generation Z.

Also, these kids want to be involved in making decisions and talking about everything, from what we eat as a family to our next vacation. Parents often find it exhausting to deal with members of Gen Z, but they need to realize that in order to teach their kids, they need to learn from them first. If we accept what they've brought with them and think about it, we'll be better parents because we'll start to question what we've always thought to be true. So, you should try to understand them and see that they are not trying to be rude.

If we accept what they've brought with them and try to figure out what it means, we'll be better parents. For the first time, we can get to the bottom of a lot of the problems.

> **"**
> *Everyone is now online, so we need to talk about real ways to raise responsible digital citizens, with a focus on digital well-being and online safety.*
> **"**

Age Orientation For Parents Raising Gen Z

There are certainly some important lessons you need to know about raising Gen Z based on the age of your child. As a parent, there is a curriculum to follow as your child advances in age.

From Ages 0 To 3

Parents with children in this age range need to be scouts. You need to observe what your child is doing and pick up on those signals. Your ability to interpret those signals accurately is key to understanding your child. Unfortunately, not many of us can do that.

From Ages 4 To 7

At this age, you are supposed to be a model. This is the age where you model competence, character, and values for your children. Additionally, you need to model for them through your lifestyle, because they learn from what they see you do.

From Ages 7 To 9

At this level, you are to be an instructor. At this age, you have to force-feed them information that will build on what you've seen from ages 0 to 3.

From Ages 10 To 12

You are supposed to be a friend; at that age, many of us lose our children because you think they can take care of themselves. However, this is the age when parents need to be their friends and converse with them about everything. It is when they should be free to learn things from you and you also learn from them.

From Ages 13 To 18

You are supposed to be a coach; at the level of a coach, you are no longer enforcing things, you are balancing perspectives. But if you don't manage the transition from friendship to coaching, you are going to lose them because they won't come to you.

At Age 19

The important lesson you need to know by this age is that you are now a cheerleader or technical advisor. At this age, your teenagers are no longer obliged to obey you, and it is the past relationship that you have cultivated with them that will carry you through.

Gen Z is easily distracted, so it's important for parents to teach them that even the best people fail sometimes, so they should learn to stick to their goals. They need to imbibe the ability to set a goal and stick to it, even when they don't feel like it. This is because great people are those who have learned to stay consistent and persistent when it comes to attaining their goals.

It is important for parents to give examples of some people who have become successful, and they should not neglect to highlight the times they have also failed. There are those who failed many times but were persistent; this will help them understand that failure is not bad.

Also, parents can unknowingly undermine their children a bit more than encourage them. The way you respond to your child can help them further develop a growth mindset.

If you are a parent of "Generation Z," then you may very well know a few things about this generation by now. They are smart. Actually, they're smarter than you; emotionally, intellectually, and spiritually.

They know a lot, courtesy of exposure to the whole world via the Internet.

They won't follow or obey anyone blindly (and that includes you as their parents), as you might have done as a child. They're going to question every rule book, every authority, and even old traditions.

The good news is that this is not all bad. This is part of a greater evolution, and it is really good for us humans too. Trust me. These children can think beyond themselves, beyond society's limiting thought process. They are more concerned about the environment, about their higher purpose and the planet, than their parents were. They are knowledgeable, practical, and mature (if you doubt it, ask your 13 or 15-year old something you didn't know at their age).

They are more collaborative than competitive (unless we force them into a cut-throat competition).

If you are a smart parent of this generation, then you know "they are here to thrive, not merely survive."

Characteristics of Parents Who Will Effectively Lead Generation Z

They Are Not Hypocrites

These parents know that their daughters and sons follow their example and advice.

They know that if they say one thing and do the other, these children will immediately catch them right away and won't even hesitate to call them hypocrites to their faces.

So, the successful parents of this generation can only lead by example.

They talk to them about things, being aware that they are talking to individuals who have minds of their own, and come to a decision that works for both parties.

They Are Not Authoritarian And Not Permissive As Well

They know that authority will only evoke rebellion and unwanted behavior in their children.

So, they learn to be patient. They tend to listen to and understand their children. This helps children understand the perspectives their parents are speaking from.

They Don't Unnecessarily Pamper And Spoil Their Kids

They realize that comfort and luxury are not going to help their children in life, but emotional resilience and mental strength will. So, they don't focus only on giving material comfort to their children, but rather they focus on cultivating inner strength and a strong family value system.

They Are Not Rigid - They Learn To Be Flexible

These parents accept the fact that times have changed. They know that their children might do things that they themselves would've never even imagined, even in their wildest fantasies.

Whether it's about their clothes or fashion choices, where to live, or pursuing their hobby as a career, they prepare themselves to accept their children and support them too.

They Don't Disrespect And Treat Their Children As Less Than Them

These parents respect their children. They know that these children have a mind of their own. They have strong opinions. They allow their children to put forward their point of view and try to be nonjudgmental about their views. They respect their thinking and choices, even if they don't agree. That way, they connect and bond with their children deeply and are able to positively influence them too.

They Know Parenting Is Not Just To Raise Their Children, But For Their Own Self-Growth

They focus on their own inner work and growth.

These parents know that in order to stay connected with these smart children, they need to up their game. That means they can't just focus on external growth like career, finances, and status.

They know that they need to grow mentally and emotionally. They must be more aware of their feelings and must also be able to choose how to act instead of just reacting to life.

They are willing to reflect, learn, and grow all the time so that they can be the best versions of themselves.

They Don't Constantly Hover Over Their Children

They create a healthy inner and outer space, which means that they know their child is not an extension of themselves, but rather they are separate individuals with their unique soul, journey, and challenges.

So, they don't constantly tell their children what to do and what not to do. Rather, they set a good example, create a healthy environment at home and let them flourish with love and acceptance. They allow children to make mistakes and learn from them. They don't react with 'I told you so'. All in all, they know parenting is a process of learning and growing along with their children. And they are a work in progress.

Think about it this way: Gen Z cares as much about emotional stability as many generations before them cared about financial stability. Think about some of the decisions we've seen.

The Gen Z population's love-life integration will be more about respecting their decision. It will also be about you supporting their mental health, providing meaningful outlets for them and the things they are passionate about in society, and making space for them to really express themselves.

Expect Accountability

It's beneficial to leave the egos at the door. You're not the only one who'll be holding someone accountable in this relationship. They will be holding you accountable just as much as you will be holding them accountable. Many parents or academics think this is a very backwards way of thinking for Gen Z, but the truth is clear.

Let's consider the case of one of my clients:

Miss Gibson came to my office with her Gen Z daughter, Princess. Miss Gibson was a divorcee who was trying to enter into a new relationship. Everything going on in her life was open to her daughter because they were very good friends. However, their relationship started to get sour when her mother started dating a new man.

In the session with Princess, she explained how her mother had given her laid-down rules on the kind of guy she should date. Her mother seemed to have forgotten, but she did not.

Princess explained how her past relationship went bad because she was considering her mother's reaction to the guy she was dating. She eventually broke up with her ex because of her mother's body language.

She was introduced to her mother's new boyfriend, and that started a series of arguments. Her mother's new boyfriend did not fit into the laid-down rules on dating that her mother had given her to follow. Yet her mother said this man was the best guy she had met yet, and she was not ready to let go of the relationship. So, Princess decided to get back with her ex-boyfriend.

During my conversation with Miss Gibson, I gave her an evaluation of what started the problem.

Her Gen Z daughter was holding her accountable, but she didn't see it happening. She didn't think there would be a time when her daughter would react to her because of her choice.

In our own generation, our parents were able to do whatever they wanted. They sort of had the "they are parents" cover, but this generation is not having it. So don't think you can give them rules for staying accountable when you will not be.

I usually tell my children before they head out of the house to call me once they arrive at their destination. My wife is typically the person I call to give an update about my whereabouts. There was a day my phone was off and I wasn't able to do this. I got home and was welcomed by my wife and children.

Then my son confronted me, saying, "Dad, you didn't call Mom. That was wrong."

And I quickly explained, "My phone battery was completely discharged and I didn't have a means to power it."

They have seen a lot of distrust in people online. They can't have that at home. You can expect Gen Z to be responsible because they don't trust power structures or the people in charge. This distrust is fueled by fake news and social media. Their doubts about the sincerity or real intentions of those in power have made them act as watchdogs. As a person of authority in their lives, they expect you to be fact-checked, and you may be met with skepticism until proven right through action.

Additionally, general societal issues like politics and gun violence heavily dictate the level of responsibility Gen Z puts on leaders. This generation feels more stressed about these issues than other generations. Because of these stressful situations, they are also more likely to have direct mental and physical health problems.

For this reason, they place accountability at the feet of their leaders to fix these issues. They look for people who do things that are controversial in society and who really care about the harm that is done to others. Generation Z will hold you accountable for what you do and say in situations like these as their parents.

As a parent and leader of Gen Z, you may not understand the intricacies of difference, the appropriate use of language, or even the rationale behind things like equity. But Gen Z has revealed that they are ready to teach! This is where the tips we talked about previously will show their significance, putting yourself in the learner's seat when you're Gen Z requires you to. Again, set the egos aside, admit your knowledge gaps, and be open to listening to them so as to be able to lead them.

Expect The Need For Financial Freedom

While Gen Z is socially conscious, morally passionate, and ethically driven, they are also about what they've affectionately dubbed "the money bag." According to the Urban Institute, Gen Zers are actually more concerned about financial freedom at a much younger age than Millennials, especially during the pandemic.

While Millennials are known for "investing" in extravagant experiences, Generation Z seems to be far more concerned with financial security, surviving an anticipated recession, and not being like their older Millennial siblings and cousins living with their parents post-graduation.

As parents of Gen Zers, we need to know about their drive to rid themselves of emotional stressors. It does not only include societal pressures, but issues related to finances as well. We, as parents, should be able to help them out by providing needed resources and advice when necessary.

Let Them Stretch Their Wings

All children deserve a varied experience, and Gen Zers are no exception. They crave knowledge from anywhere and will absorb what's happening around them.

Open the doors for them to explore subjects such as architecture, performing arts, nature, other cultures, culinary arts, and more. Let them try "adult" things, whether at home or with your business. For instance, my son helps with our lawn and assists his mum in arranging the interior of our home. He's able to apply his interests to decisions left to the parents. In encouraging this, we're letting him know we take his interests seriously (and, as an added bonus, our home is wonderfully decorated).

Allow Them To Learn In A Relevant Space

The space in which young adults reside and learn has changed. Gen Zers no longer have brick-and-mortar boundaries. Instead of heading to the library for information or the classified section to look for jobs, they're turning to their smartphones (which a whopping 96 percent of them own and which is one reason the Google algorithm favors mobile sites).

Their existence includes social media and virtual engagements—things we as parents didn't have growing up. Although reading news stories on Twitter or looking for work on Facebook's job boards might not sound normal to parents, it's important to allow children to find information in spaces they enjoy and thrive in, no matter how nontraditional it seems.

Don't write off social media as a time waster. Alternatively, ask your children how they're getting their information. What do they read, and what do they do with that information? You'll be working to understand their world (and even learn alongside them) while granting them the freedom to learn in a way that works for them.

Let Them Fail. Please!

Risk-taking is essential, and many have worried that Millennials are too cushioned by their parents. Gen Zers need to make mistakes, and parents need to allow them to do that. If your child doesn't make the soccer team, for instance, resist the urge to speak with the coach. Instead, let your Gen Zer speak to the coach himself to figure it out on his own. Let them face the consequences of their mistake and fix it.

Don't always be in a haste to fix all their problems for them. Some Millennials are unable to do much or anything for themselves because they have been helped their entire lives. By the time a parent is ready to take their hands off fixing things for their kids, certain habits have been formed. The habits will in turn affect the other parts of their lives.

It's natural to worry that children will feel alone without a safety net, but some parents' actions have been shown to have negative effects. Psychology Today reports that young adults with overly involved parents have greater chances of developing anxiety or depression. Kids crave independence, so grant them some, even if it means they'll hit setbacks.

You've probably got your own ideas about the issues your Gen Zer is dealing with (especially when it comes to school), but don't rely too heavily on your own experience to guide your parenting.

GenZers don't enjoy antiquated anecdotes. They want answers that are meaningful to their own realities, and that means accepting that their obstacles do not necessarily mirror yours.

Instead, acknowledge that their world is different from yours when you were their age and listen to what's troubling them without judgment. Adulthood in general, and starting a job, is both exciting and hard. During this time, you want to make sure you're helping your Gen Zers and not pushing them away.

How to Support Your Entrepreneurial Kids

Your children might live in a different age, but the reward of feeling happy and successful at work—a reward you, as an entrepreneur, are well familiar with—is one thing that won't change from generation to generation.

As Generation Z enters the workforce, you can share your knowledge with them, recognize the generational differences and help them set goals they can be proud of achieving.

CHAPTER TEN
Disciplining Them

I am a member of Generation X, as are nearly all of the leaders in our life coaching network. I belong to a generation with certain characteristics. We are:

Hardworking

Self-Assured

Competitive

Goal-centric

Resourceful

Mentally focused

Team-oriented

Independent

Disciplined

In my network, at my workplace, and on the committees to which I belong, the majority of our leaders began as students attending various conferences with mentors who kept track of their lives.

These mentors became more like second parents who, for the most part, knew how to give punishments and rewards when they were needed. I certainly have this experience, as I have worked with kids for years and continue to do so.

In the past decade, something has changed

We observe that fewer students are willing to assume leadership roles, fewer students settle in the city after graduation, and fewer students are eager to have others "speak into" their lives.

When we started to look into this problem, it became clear that this is a major trait of Generation Z, which is often called neurotic. They are self-centered and surgically attached to their phones. My millennial mentees did not respond the same way to the rhythms of discipline I had taught them.

> **"**
> *Your child has to see and understand clearly that he is deserving of the discipline meted out to him each time.* **"**

The following are strategies I've used with my Gen Z mentees and children:

Develop Trust

Millennials, from our perspective, desired direction and enjoyed engaging dialogue. Leadership was eagerly listened to. This was not the case for Generation Z. When I tried to talk to Gen Z the same way I talked to Millennials, I made some big mistakes.

According to statistics, Gen Z grows up slower than Millennials, experiencing rites of passage at a later age. On average, a student entering university now is three years younger than I was when I started school.

Gen Z is wary of "authority" and seeks a broader range of authority figures. As a parent, your voice is one of many, and if you are the only one expressing something different, you are weighed appropriately. You must learn how to earn people's trust. Yes! Build trust and then rebuild it; this is what will make discipline easier when the time comes.

Your youngster must see and understand that he is deserving of the penalties that are meted out to him when he gets them. We have been able to construct successful partnerships by gradually developing genuine, trusting ties. My Gen Z friends and children are far more inclined to listen to me and trust me if they know I adore them.

Withdraw Access To Technology Temporarily

Instead of yelling at your children, which I highly discourage, limiting their access to technology is one way to discipline them for their excesses. I adore technology, don't get me wrong, but we're beginning to realize that it isn't always beneficial.

Generation Z is the first generation to grow up in the digital age. The fact that technology is everywhere can be seen to affect people's anxiety, attention spans, and social skills.

Since Generation Z lives in this world, I don't think that telling them to get rid of their smartphones will work. We must discover ways to educate them.

Because this generation has become addicted to technology, it is one of the best ways to punish them. Technology is both their strength and potential weakness.

Depending on its application, one of the things I do with my children at home is restrict their internet and phone usage for a period of time. Based on the severity of the offense. And you can try it on your children, since it works miracles.

Frequently, many parents state that they have grounded their children as a form of punishment, but these children have cell phones and computers in their rooms. You simply provided them with a mini-vacation.

These children will not leave their rooms because the people with whom they wish to contact are readily accessible on their mobile devices.

You've just made it possible for them to do more of the things they enjoy doing on the phone or computer, whichever they choose. Consequently, you will discover that the child you disciplined yesterday is still doing the same thing he was punished for. So, the right way to use technology to discipline children is to make sure they can't connect to the internet when they're being punished.

> *Because technology has become like a form of addiction to these ones, it is one of the best things to use as punishment.*

Involve Them In Question-Based Conversations

Before punishing people from Generation Z, it's usually a good idea to come to an agreement. Together, you and your child must reach a point where he realizes he deserves to be punished. Before administering discipline, you must initiate a discourse based on questions. This question-based conversation is meant to find out what the child was thinking when he didn't follow the given order.

Occasionally, I have learned through dialogue that my child attempted to do something positive but failed. Even though it looks like he did something wrong, I won't punish him or her if his or her goal and reason for doing it are good. But consider how my child will see me if I immediately administer punishment. This by itself will have an effect on our connection.

Occasionally, I observe my child engaging in activities that I consider unproductive. I begin by posing questions. Do you know how much your time is worth in the marketplace if you spend all day playing video games? The goal is to get them to see that playing video games all day is not a good thing.

What do you think the outcome would be if you were the father in this house and spent this amount of time playing and having fun?

I will even detail a few of the costs associated with maintaining the house as we do. I occasionally incorporate tuition and basic expenses into my conversations with my child. How much game time do you believe you would receive if you were in my position?

I then proceeded to counsel my child.

I do not simply reprimand them and leave it at that. The child must understand where he went wrong and what he needs to do to make amends during the reprimand. Occasionally, highlighting the problem alone is what causes additional problems. But helping the child understand where he went wrong makes him realize he has acted improperly.

There must be a purpose for reprimanding a Generation Z child. It cannot be that you intend for him or her to feel horrible. If this is why you reprimand, then you are performing a poor job. The child should feel remorse for his or her wrongdoing and learn from the correction how to behave properly.

Be Firm And Uncompromising

I am familiar with how you feel when you are with your child. They are our jewels, and we will always treat them with care. However, being excessively sensitive and compromising can lead to greater problems in the future. Because our interactions with our children can teach them how to interact with others in the world. In fact, it is essential that they be punished when they deserve it.

Punishment is an integral aspect of love. When you love a child, you will discipline him or her. And children build habits based on how we interact with them as they develop. Imagine constantly covering up for your child or never correcting them when necessary. They do not eventually recognize that they are mistaken. And this is precisely how they will interact with their children. Due to how they see your dispute with them, they may at times question your affection for them, but they must never question your honesty or the reason they are disciplined.

CONCLUSION

So, What Makes Gen Z Different?

The best answers to this question will help parents guide and aid their children to reach their full potential.

As people in this generation get older, they go to college, get jobs, and take on more responsibilities in our society. We shall continue to observe them in order to comprehend them as parents.

In the first part of this book, I talked more about how different each generation is. In our multigenerational society, parents and children perceive the world differently. The grandparents also don't understand why "this generation's youth" do not seem to value the amount of knowledge they have.

In part two, we looked at how Generation Z is different in terms of relationships, jobs, and money. Generation Z is very outspoken and direct about how they disagree with social norms and don't want to follow the pattern of finding love, getting married, and having kids.

Gen Z is the generation with the most relaxed attitude toward the major life events of having children and getting married, despite the fact that individuals of earlier generations have chosen not to have children and/or get married.

They are slow to commit because they like to test the waters and look at all their options before settling down. In some cases, they do this even after settling down, while they are still getting financially independent.

Generation Z is different from previous generations, so their goals and expectations for themselves are also different. This generation, which grew up during a time of fast technological growth, has its own standards and objectives when it comes to choosing a workplace and employment.

While every generation is unique in its own way when it comes to money and finance, the Z generation appears to be the one that will revolutionize the world of finance.

This generation must be able to adjust in order to deal with problems that both the current generation and the generation before it have caused. The unusual aspect, however, is that they are adapting and acclimating considerably faster than expected.

Generation Z experiences worries and problems inherited from previous generations. Many of them saw their parents, who were part of Generation X, have trouble making ends meet because of the Great Recession.

Even though many of them had stable jobs and a lot of money, they couldn't make it through the economic storm.

Gen Z also saw how hard it was for Millennials to get used to new technology when it came out. They saw what happened to people's money when they put more value on spending than saving and didn't think about the effects of their choices.

These experiences significantly shape Gen Z's understanding of money and financial literacy.

In the third section, I talk about how I've worked with many teachers, therapists, psychologists, parents, and people who are about to become parents. I've talked about the best ways for parents and other important people to raise Generation Z.

Aside from being essence seekers, this generation differs from the rest of us.

Gen Z strives ceaselessly to discover and express their true identities. Growing up in a culture that is not necessarily at its best shaped a generation that does not appreciate sugar-coating or rose-colored glasses. In their never-ending search for authenticity, Generation Z's life goals have become more realistic and their place in society has become more progressive. This is because they feel empowered by their peers and are driven by a sense of purpose.

Reality Shifters

Generation Z takes a flexible approach to life because they see the world as something that can't be fixed. In today's culture, looking for the truth and wanting to make things better are not all linear processes. No, Generation Z believes that people's realities (and reality in general) are fluid and constantly changing. Generation Z is not afraid to draw outside the lines to show how creative they are.

Their very creative spirits have been set free by their desire to learn more about who they really are, find ways to bring about change, and try out different ways to express themselves. Social media has made it easier for Gen Z to explore and try new things by giving them a nearly endless creative sandbox and a critical mass of people with similar interests with whom to connect.

AFTERWORD

It has been said that it takes a whole village to raise a child, but I will beg to slightly differ on this notion. The village concept has moved from what it used to be. The village has gone virtual. It now takes a deep understanding of how the world of children operates to effectively raise one.

The age-long concern and question of every parent and guardian I have met in my over 30 years of ministry, mentoring, and relationship coaching, is about the best ways to understand, relate to, and raise the next generation. While there are many literary works attempting to offer answers, few of them have realistically addressed the issue. The real answers are not far away from everyone again.

To effectively raise the next generation, we must relate well with them. In order to relate well with them, we must fully understand them. The part of the equation that has to do with understanding them seems to be mysterious and herculean to average parents and guardians. That's where this masterpiece from Ben comes into play.

The whole idea of "What Makes Gen-Z Different?" is to help you, as the reader, fully comprehend how the world of Generation Z kids works. They are completely different from the previous generations. The system of raising them too has changed. It's a different world.

Ben has been my protégé and media advisor for over two decades. His passion for the younger generation is relentless. He is a man of great influence and significance, well-versed and experienced in raising the next generation. This book combines both his adept aptitude and first-hand experience as a father to Generation Z and the Alpha Generation.

The problem of "not knowing how to" is now solved through the insights Ben has outlined in this book – What Makes Gen-Z Different.

- Dr. Amos Fenwa
Family Life & Relationship Coach

ACKNOWLEDGMENT

Putting my years of experience and findings about a generation that's uniquely different into a book wouldn't have been possible without the collective efforts and support of several people. A simple "thank you" seems insufficient because it may not fully express my depth of gratitude. It really would take writing an entire book to even begin to express my gratitude to everyone who has been so helpful to me. But permit me to mention just a few names here.

First, to my family, I say a huge thank you. This is not just a routine greeting. I'm indeed grateful given how much I have learned and gleaned from my wife Dorcas, as co-parent, and our kids, who are Gen-Z and Alpha. The weekly conversation with my boys over the years and frequent playtime with my girl has given me so much insight into their world. Thank you, Jesse, Theo and Anita, for being the best kids.

Teeman Tobi-Adebowale and the editorial team at Teeman Studios, I appreciate you guys. Thank you, Evans Okunola for making the connection with this team possible. You all midwifed the book with so much intentionality and professionalism.

I say thank you to my parents (both Baby Boomers) and my siblings (Gen-X & Millennials). They helped shape the successful Gen-X I have become. Thank you, Debbie, Kenny,

Taiwo (my armorbearer), Bishop and Bukky – you guys are the best. To my big brother and his family—Ps. Victor Ogungbemi, thank you for the love and support.

To Dr. Amos Fenwa, my mentor of over 20 years, I appreciate your continuous encouragement and writing the afterword. Also, to my friend and sister – Issata O., for painstakingly reading the manuscripts and writing the foreword. I appreciate Tayo, Manny and Tise. To Dr. Joseph Siju PhD and his lovely wife, Lolade, thank you for giving me the opportunity to share the ideas behind this book at the IMPACT2022 Conference.

To the entire families at Jubilee Place Voorhees NJ, House of Stars Union NJ, GPA Houston TX, GICC Upper Marlboro MD and HCC Global, it's been a great honor to work with everyone over the years.

Finally, I want to specially appreciate all the parents, guardians, teachers, counselors and younger folks I have worked with in the last twenty years plus.

REFERENCES

Prakash, R. (2018, September 12). Role of the Family in a Child's Development. Retrieved from https://parenting.firstcry.com/articles/role-of-family-in-childs-development.

Dimock, M. (2019, January 17). Defining generations: Where Millennials end and Generation Z begins. Retrieved from https://www.pewresearch.org/about

Jagaciak, A. (2017, July 10). Shifts from Generation Y to Generation Z. Retrieved from https://medium.com/the-future-of-things/shifts-from-generation-y-to-generation-z-43c353730b72

Stillman, D. (2019, November 14). Generation Z Statistics That Can Make or Break Your Business. Retrieved from https://genguru.com/generation-z-statistics

Contreras, M. Equality in LGBT community. Retrieved from https://podcasts.apple.com/us/podcast/equality-in-lgbt-community-montse-contreras-dani-chávez/id1566955656

Bizouati-Kennedy, Y. (2022, March 24). Quitting Your Job in Under a Year Is Not the Resume 'Red Flag' It Once Was Thanks to COVID. Retrieved from https://finance.yahoo.com/news/quitting-job-under-not-resume-180534788.html

"5 Things Pharmaceutical Recruiters Need to Know About Gen Z." medreps.com. https://www.medreps.com/medical-sales-careers/what-pharmaceutical-recruiters-need-to-know-about-gen-z

"Your Guide to Gen Z: 3 Common Misconceptions." memberclicks.com. https://memberclicks.com/blog/your-guide-to-gen-z-3-common-misconceptions

"Is it time for your kid to have a phone?" lobservateur.com. https://www.lobservateur.com/2019/08/24/is-it-time-for-your-kid-to-have-a-phone.

"Social media facts & advice." internetmatters.org. https://www.internetmatters.org/resources/social-media-advice-hub/social-media-benefits.

Bryne, J. (2022, March 1). GEN-Z Relationship with Romance is a complex one. Retrieved from https://medium.com/@bdajess/gen-zs-relationship-with-romance-is-a-complex-one-69ca1184d4c4

"is the 'Big Quit' over? April 20, 2022." thehouston100.com. https://thehouston100.com/business/2022/04/20/is-the-big-quit-over/14939

"Is Your Workplace Ready to Welcome Technology-Savvy Gen Z?." empxtrack.com. https://empxtrack.com/blog/gen-z (accessed September 22, 2022).

SAMANTHA, (2021, October 22). The Talking Stage: What Is It & How to Progress to the Next One. Retrieved from https://www.lovepanky.com/flirting-flings/dating-game/talking-stage

RUTH IGIELNIK, K. (2022, October 22). On the Cusp of

Adulthood and Facing an Uncertain Future: What We Know About Gen Z So Far. Retrieved from https://www.pewresearch.org/social-trends/2020/05/14/on-the-cusp-of-adulthood-and-facing-an-uncertain-future-what-we-know-about-gen-z-so-far-2/

Harrison, L. (2021, February 22). Gen Z has a major fear of commitment, it's not our fault. Retrieved from https://phsprecedent.com/showcase/2021/11/01/gen-z-has-a-major-fear-of-commitment-and-its-not-our-fault/

Blake, R. (2022, October 22). Young People Prioritize Financial Matters, in Their Own Way. Retrieved from https://portfolio.bisanet.org/Article/young-people-prioritize-financial-matters-in-their-own-way

Lee, E. (2020, December 17). Here's the Definitive Data Behind How Gen Z and Millennials Meet and Fall in Love. Retrieved from https://www.theknot.com/content/gen-z-relationships-marriage